AF541162

TEACHING, LEARNING AND CURRICULUM

TEACHING, LEARNING AND CURRICULUM

By

Prof. Marlow Ediger

B.S.E., M.A, Ed.D. (Education)
Emeritus Professor of Education
Truman State University
201 West 22nd Street
North Newton KS 67117
United States of America
mediger2@cox.net

&

Prof. Digumarti Bhaskara Rao

M.Sc., M.A., M.A., M.Ed., Ph.D.
Dean, Faculty of Education
Member, Academic Senate
Member, Research Advisory Committee
Former Chairman, Board of Studies in Education
Acharya Nagarjuna University, Guntur
External Member, Board of Studies in Education
Adikavi Nannaya University, Rajahmundry
External Member, Board of Studies in Education
Vikrama Simhapuri University, Nellore
External Member, Board of Studies in Special Education
Member, Departmental Research Committee in Education
Krishna University, Machilipatnam
Corresponding Address
D-43, SVN Colony, Guntur 522006, Andhra Pradesh, (India)
digumartibhaskararao@rediffmail.com
+91-9493333555 & 8500114411

DISCOVERY PUBLISHING HOUSE PVT. LTD.
NEW DELHI-110 002

Published by:
Namit Wasan

DISCOVERY PUBLISHING HOUSE PVT. LTD.
4383/4B, Ansari Road, Darya Ganj
New Delhi-110 002 (India)
Phone : +91-11-23279245, 43596064-65
Fax : +91-11-23253475
E-mail : discoverypublishinghouse@gmail.com
namitwasan9@gmail.com
sales@discoverypublishinggroup.com
web : www.discoverypublishinggroup.com

First Edition: 2016

ISBN: 978-93-5056-793-7

Teaching, Learning and Curriculum

Printed at:
Infinity Imaging Systems
Delhi

Dedicated to

Gadde Mangaiah

Preface

Teaching is the imparting of knowledge by a knowledgeable teacher to the unknowledgeable students. Learning is an act of acquiring or modifying or reinforcing the new existing knowledge, behaviours, skills, values, or preferences and may involve synthesizing different types of information. Curriculum is broadly defined as the totality of student experiences that occur in the educational process.

The curriculum is meant for effective teaching and learning. The curriculum, teaching and learning are interwoven and one cannot be separated from the other in any educational set-up. The use of curriculum that addresses the complexities of teaching and learning are explained to the best extent. Many issues and concerns concerned to teaching, learning and curriculum are discussed in detail. This book will be of great use to the curriculum specialists, textbook writers, teachers and administrators at school stages.

Digumarti Bhaskara Rao
digumartibhaskararao@rediffmail.com
Tele-Mobile +91 949 3333 555

Sri Sai Soudha
D-43, S.V.N. Colony
Guntur-522006
India

CONTENTS

CHAPTER 1
What is of Most Worth in Teaching and Learning?

John Locke (1632-1702), wrote an essay on what knowledge is of most worth in education. He placed "virtue" at the top of the list. A virtuous person is one who is a good person in society, according to Locke. He/she does not portray the likeness of persons who are evil and do unapproved things. Second in importance was "wisdom." A person filled with wisdom makes quality decisions in every day life. Third, Locke listed "breeding" as being essential. These individuals did not exhibit characteristics of "sheepish bashfulness." Being too bashful to communicate effectively hinders the individual from interacting with others. Fourth, Locke listed "knowledge" as being salient. He states being very "bookish"; but feels knowledge is fourth in importance.

Values in the Curriculum

There are a plethora of early educators who left their marks in educational theory and practice. Johann Friedrich Pestalozzi (1746-1827), brought in the object lesson whereby pupils learned initially from concrete materials before moving on to the abstract. Thus, for instance, in reading about a ball, the object would be there for learner observation and discussion. Also, school was to be a joyous place rather than where licking and learning went hand in hand in the classroom. The classroom and school environment became salient factors in pupil achievement and progress.

Friedrich Wilhelm Froebel (1782-1852), stressed the importance of kindergarten education with its activity centered approach. Creativity was a major objective in his kindergarten education plan. For example, Froebel emphasized the mother play song experience whereby pupils would stand in a circle and then creatively dramatize what was sung. If pupils sang about planting a garden, each step of planting including seeding, cultivating, hoeing, and irrigating, would be pantomimed.

Johann Friedrich Herbart (1776-1841), a leading educator who had a teacher training school, placed major emphasis upon methodology of instruction. In his lesson plans, the first step of teaching involved preparation of the student for the ensuing lesson. The step of "preparation" was actually readiness to benefit from the lesson. Step two involved presentation of the new lesson followed by step three stressing "association." Here, the pupil learned to tie together or relate the subject matter acquired with that of previous learnings. This related to forming a generalization of and from relating ideas. Otherwise too many isolated items were acquired. The last step of learning in a lesson plan to be implemented consisted of making use of subject matter learned so that forgetting would less likely occur. Retention of generalizations was then stressed (Ediger and Rao, 2000).

Bringing to bear salient events in the history of education reveals how past occurrences are utilized in part by present day educations. Thus, the following are examples:

- wisdom in becoming a moral being by Locke.
- concrete materials use in instruction by Pestalozzi.
- creativity and kindergarden education by Froebel.
- specific methods of instruction by Herbart.

Present day philosophies in education emphasize knowledge goals as being the most salient. No Child Left Behind (NCLB) tested pupils in grades three through eight in reading and the language arts as well as once on the secondary school level involving high stakes testing. These tests tended to stress the importance of knowledge and related skills to achieve knowledge. Beginning in the 2014-2015 school year, the Common Core State Standards (CCSS) will be implemented in 37 states who have signed on. Reading and mathematics still emphasize knowledge goals in CCSS. Reasons for this emphasis include the following:

- these are goals which all need to achieve to be successful in college and careers.
- essential subject matter is stressed and necessary.
- the basics are identified and need to be attained by learners.

William Chandler Bagley (1872-1946), believed and advocated that basic subject matter be identified and taught in schools; he opposed an activity centered curriculum. Bagley's essentialism, however, was broader in scope than the initial NCLB and CCSS in that it included social studies and science. Contrast the thinking of Bagley with that of the objectives stressed in importance by the National Education Association's (NEA) 1917, THE SEVEN CARDINAL PRINCIPLES OF EDUCATION and these were in the order they were broadly presented:

- health instruction.
- command of fundamental processes (subject matter knowledge).
- home membership.
- vocations.
- citizenship
- worthy use of leisure time.
- ethical character.

The scope of the above Seven Cardinal Principles of Education is much broader than NCLB or CCSS. Health education, being a good member of the home setting, vocational education, wisdom in the utilization of leisure time, as well as goals in ethics become poignant. The feeling and beliefs were that there are other salient avenues of significant learning, other than subject matter knowledge. For example, to be sure, good physical and mental health are of utmost importance to function well individually as well as of members in society.

The Educational Policies Commission (1938), of the NEA identified four major areas of objectives for pupil achievement, and these were:

- a description of the educated person, being able to solve personal problems.
- a description of the educated member of the family and community.
- a description of the educated producer or consumer.
- a description of the educated citizen (See Shepherd and Ragan, 1982).

The above asterisked items placed much emphasis upon individual development as well as being a member of society. Goals pertaining to being a member in society received little/ no stress in NCLB objectives.

In 1962, the Educational Policies Commission (NEA) came out with the Central Purpose of American Education and that being to develop individuals with thinking abilities. They emphasized that thinking should permeate all areas of the curriculum, regardless of subject matter involved. Thus, analyzing content into component parts and viewing each carefully to ascertain what is salient, important, relevant, and worthy from that of lesser value. Thus, main ideas are separated from subordinate content in problem solving. Solutions are sought for problems with analytic thought and deliberation. Thinking and problem solving are processes and a means to an end which is a solution. Too frequently, test scores or ends are sought. Focus should also be placed on the means or processes in order for quality ends to ensue. The following are reasons for focusing upon critical thinking as well as problem solving:

- they are always useful in school and in society.
- individuals are expected to solve personal and social problems.
- jumping to hasty conclusions is minimized.
- reflecting upon previous experiences assists in arriving at improved ensuing solutions to problems.

By studying what has been presented previously in terms of statements of objectives and goals from diverse organizations and rulings, one is in a better position to evaluate which ends should be stressed in the curriculum. Pupils are living in an increasingly complex society and world and need to be prepared to meet challenges of a rapidly changing environment. Being flexible and making necessary adaptations, the present and future participant in society may be in a better position to identify and solve problems. Changes which must be made include the following:

- a fair, just, and equitable society for all inhabitants.
- modifying/eliminating job and income discrimination so that poverty is a thing of the past.
- optimal achievement emphasized for each learner.

In addition, there are other equally poignant objectives for pupil achievement in an ongoing process including, self efficacy, feelings of self worth, being able to work collaboratively with others, trust, and self renewable.

REFERENCES

Ediger, Marlow, and D. Bhaskara Rao (2000), Philosophy and Curriculum. New Delhi, India, Discovery Publishing House.

Shepherd, Gene D., and William B. Ragan (1982), Modern Elementary Curriculum. New York: Holt, Rhinehart and Winston, p. 480.

CHAPTER 2
Concerns in Curriculum

There are plethora of concerns in the curriculum. Each need analyzations, indepth study, and possible solutions discovered. It behooves teachers and school supervisors to say abreast of the latest trends in curriculum development, as well as coming up with creative ways of assisting pupils to achieve more optimally. Which concerns and issues are relevant for deliberation?

Concerns and Issues in the Curriculum

A major dilemma pertains to the amount of standardized testing to emphasize. There are complaints that an excessive amount of testing is being stressed. Parents in New York city have kept children home when another standardized test has been given in the school setting. In Seattle, Washington, classroom teachers have refrained from administering a standardized test. The feelings are that too many tests are given which robs children of instructional time. With mass scoring of standardized tests, there have been many glitches in the resulting scores. Then too, teachers and administrators have changed answers on pupils answer sheets prior to their being scanned for correctness/incorrectness of answers. This has resulted in unfair practices in changing pupil test results to indicate higher scores, thus, the question arises, "How much time should be spent on testing in a school year?

Second, ways of evaluating teacher progress has become a concern. Are standardized tests a salient approach in assessing teaching performance? Most teachers are greatly opposed due to the following reasons, among others:

- there are a plethora of factors influencing test scores,

other than the quality of instruction, such as the home and community environment.

- many children come from impoverished homes and lack food, clothing, shelter, and safety needs.
- Socio-economic factors influence pupil achievement and progress (Ediger, 2009).

The business world, largely, favours testing as a means of ridding schools of bad teachers. Teachers should provide favourable test results in order to be offered a contract for the ensuing school year. They believe that heavy taxes hinder increased numbers of businesses coming into any state. Good teachers will encourage the business world to prosper and grow the economy. Questions which arise here include the following:

- which is a fair way of raising taxes to encourage high quality schools as well as social programs?
- are people merely attempting to not pay taxes, regardless of the consequences? There are many advertisements on TV in which attorneys will try to get people out of paying no or little taxes. Huge reductions or eliminations are mentioned in tax reductions by these ads.
- when taxes are reduced such as in eliminating income tax, is there a replacement for the omission? A few years ago, a group of ministers stated that sales tax on food purchases are unfair and should be omitted. Then the question arose as to which sources of revenue would take its place? This idea was soon dropped in eliminating sales tax on food items (Ediger, 2014).

Public schools depend upon tax moneys, and there is no way around supporting its endeavours with collection plate money.

Fourth, who should appraise teaching performance? There are advocates that school principals should have that responsibility. Any teacher deemed incapable needs to be replaced. Should school principals then possess the power to hire and fire teachers? Principals need to be properly educated to assume this grave responsibility, if it be given. Schools of education at universities should then train, principals for this task. They need to be keen observers of teaching performance as well as possess relevant criteria for assessment. Criteria such as the following are relevant in that teachers should:

- possess capabilities of involving all pupils in learning.
- attempt to secure interests of learners.
- develop perceived purpose within pupils.
- assist pupils to attach meaning to facts, concepts, and
- vary the types of experiences provided to keep pupils on task.

School principals must treat teachers fairly, without hatred and biased favouritism. Principal evaluation of teachers will fail if they are vindictive, rude, and desire loyalty as their only goal in the evaluation process.

Fifth, how should schools of education at universities educate prospective teachers in light of Common Core State Standards emphasis in the public schools? Should professors of education then stress how prospective teachers should achieve these objectives in teaching and learning situations? Not all states in the union, of course, have subscribed to stressing these objectives. Some have backed out, leaving 37 states presently. Then too, how long will CCSS be in endurance in that a new plan might then be emphasized? The writer is 86 years of age and has experienced many plans of instruction since his beginning as a teacher in 1951. At that time, the concept of "accountability" was not in vogue and in the two teacher school, no mandated tests were required. To graduate from grade school in 1942, the county school system required the taking of essay tests in social studies, reading/literature, mathematics, and spelling. Social Studies received the most emphasis in terms of the total test score. Science was not tested upon and received little emphasis in the curriculum. Spelling was very salient. Toward the end of each school year, the top spellers in a school competed in the local county spelling contest. The writer still has a red ribbon for being the second best speller in his grade level.

Even in 1955-61, no mandated tests were required in these smaller rural schools. Having taught abroad in the Hashemite Kingdom of the Jordan, 1952-54, as a parochial classroom teacher, the writer only experienced the writing of his own tests for students in the classroom setting. An issue and concern which arises then pertains to how much standardized testing should be stressed as compared to teacher written tests? Moore emphasis must be placed within inservice education in the writing of test items which are valid and reliable.

Sixth, there is an increased need to do a better job of teaching English Language Learners (ELL). The test results of ELL students were disaggregated from the others in terms of results from No Child Left Behind. Children who speak another language, in whole or in part in the home setting, need adequate consideration in terms of objectives to be achieved, learning opportunities to attain the chosen ends, as well as appraisal procedures. They can become valuable contributors in society once the vocabulary and sentence structure of the English language is mastered. ELL must be educated to the point whereby they become contributing members in society as well as grow in the direction of self fulfillment. Respect and acceptance are poignant concepts to remember in teaching and learning situations. These learners need teaching and supervision whereby they attain and achieve as optimally as possible. But, this is true in teaching all children in any classroom including the mentally impaired as well as other handicapped children.

In Closing

All pupils need to experience a high quality curriculum which provides for individual differences in the classroom. Each needs to have personal needs met, including feelings of belonging and esteem provisions. The school curriculum must be developed so that it:

- is motivational for all learners.
- provides for the interests of pupils.
- assists pupils to perceive purpose in achievement.
- injects meaning and understanding of subject matter content.

REFERENCES

Ediger, Marlow (2009), "Issues in the Social Studies," Experiments in Education, 37 (4), 75-78.

Ediger, Marlow (2014), "Assisting Pupils in Learning in the Classroom," Research and Pedagogic Interventions, 3 (1), 9-15.

CHAPTER 3

Sequence in Curriculum

Sequence in learning is a very salient concept in teaching and learning situations. Pupils need to experience high quality learning activities which build upon previous knowledge and skills acquired, otherwise learning might become too easy/ boring or too complex whereby the learner loses out on achieving objectives of instruction. Thus, the teacher needs to be highly cognizant of order in providing activities and experiences for pupils. Pupils must interact with the learning opportunities provided in which they become actively involved; otherwise minimal learning will occur. Sequence then becomes a major concept to keep in mind permanently when teaching pupils.

Sequential Experiences for Pupils

Johann Friedrich Herbart (1776-1841), was an early educator who developed the idea of lesson plans to stress what an ensuing plan of instruction should look like. Herbart had his own teacher training school whereby preservice teachers were educated to use a specific procedure in teaching. There were general steps involved in the daily lesson plan, which included the following:

- **Preparation:** Here, the teacher reviewed with pupils what was taught previously. This brought to children's attention, knowledge already acquired. Readiness for the new learnings was being emphasized.
- **Presentation:** The next step in teaching, involved the actual teaching of subject matter, directly based on the step of preparation. With adequate background information, the pupil is to relate the new with the old. Thus, subject matter is not taught in isolation, but indicates its relationship in sequence.

- **Association:** The teacher is to help pupils make associations between the two steps of learning. Subject matter is retained longer with pupils making the connections.
- **Generalization:** In connecting the steps of presentation with that of association, a generalization is realized. Too many bits of information might be learned unless a broader statement of objectives is achieved, that being the generalization.
- **Application:** Being able to apply what has been learned makes subject matter useful and aids in retention (Ediger and Rao, 2003).

Herbart stressed the importance of quality sequence in history and literature, although it is applicable in other curriculum areas.

Jerome Bruner (1922-), Professor of Education at Harvard University, emphasized a spiral curriculum in sequential learnings. The spiral curriculum stressed pupils making revisits as learning progressed. Thus within a unit of study, the pupil has opportunities to review briefly what had been studied previously, and then move sequentially to more complex ordered subject matter.

Structural ideas would generally be selected by academicians in their respective areas of specialization. Thus, for example, historians would carefully identify key ideas for pupils to achieve inductively. These are the broader concepts and generalizations of the historical/social studies unit being taught. Teachers then may choose learning activities for pupil interaction to attain the stated objectives. A variety of experiences would be involved which might well stress involved pupils working as historians with, for example, using primary and secondary sources of information, among others. To achieve the structural ideas and their subordinate content, pupils. would be evaluated in terms of their attainment of major ideas, subordinate content directly related to the structure, as well as related relevant details. To do this, pupils would revisit at intervals in the spiral curriculum. Induction is a method of learning. What are the advantages of Jerome Bruner's spiral curriculum?

- there is a generalized approach with guidelines in ascertaining sequence using a spiral curriculum.
- revisits stress the saliency of retention of subject matter through review or presentation of previous content in a different way.
- structural ideas provide standards for the importance of choosing relevant content to teach.
- inductive approaches are fascinating and generally appreciated by pupils as a methodology of instruction.

Constructivism as a psychology/philosophy of learning stresses the significance of having pupils sequence their own progress with teacher assistance as needed. A project method, stressing constructivism, is a recognized procedure in teaching and learning situations whereby the teacher is a helper, consultant and guide in assisting learners in ongoing activities. William Heard Kilpatrick (1874-1965), late Professor of Columbia University, was an early advocate of the project method. In it, he emphasized that pupils become independent and autonomous in curriculum endeavours. Broad standards were described in assisting pupils in the project method of instruction. These were the following:

- **Pupils having a purpose:** Here, pupils within an ongoing unit of study, perceived intrinsic reasons for engaging in the activity. The teacher's role was to motivate and encourage pupils in identifying a worthwhile project. Clarity in accepting the purpose was a necessity, whereas wholehearted involvement propelled learners to proceed with the purpose or project.
- **Planning:** Definite plans need to be made within a committee to collaborate in doing the project. This still leaves much room for pupil considerations as the project unfolds. Pupil involvement in all phases of project development is important in learning by doing.
- **Executing or carrying out the plans to fruition:** Collaboratively, learners were actively engaged in the project and sequenced their very own work. With teacher

help, pupils are able to go ahead on their own and assist each other in a cooperative manner. Meticulous work is desired and what is worth doing is worth doing well. Materials and reference sources, as needed, are at the committees disposal.

- **Judging:** The ongoing and completed project needs evaluation in terms of desired standards. Committee members with the teachers assistance must develop criteria for judging the complete project. Learners need to learn to do standards to appraise, and this is a salient part of the project method. As objectively as possible, the project's merits and weaknesses need to be assessed. Self evaluation becomes increasingly salient in the lives of individuals and the project method allows time for this endeavor (Wahlquist, 1942).

With constructivists' philosophy/psychology, the learner is throughly involved in achieving goals of instruction. The focal point is upon the learner in teaching and learning situations. He/she must do the learning in a wholehearted manner and do this in an independent manner, as much as possible. Autonomy in achieving is salient in ongoing experiences.

William Chandler Bagley (1874-1946) was a strong advocate of the basics in the curriculum. He opposed the activity centered approach in instructional procedures, rather a strong academic curriculum was advocated. Bagley believed strongly in stressing each academic discipline separate from the others with little/no integration of content to be taught. History, for example, should be taught separately as an academic discipline. Learning should be rigorous due to life in and of itself having numerous responsibilities. Thus, a sink full of dishes needs to be washed if liking it or not te involved. This is not to say that life is drudgery, but it does have things which need to be accomplished, remedied, and taken care of. The teacher then must choose objectives for each academic discipline when teaching pupils. The objectives, selected, must be ordered or sequenced properly.

Behaviorism is very much in vogue presently with its emphasis upon precise, measurably stated objectives of instruction which leave little/no room for interpretation. The objectives may be mandated or teacher determined. Generally, they are state mandated for pupil achievement in the classroom. Sequential achievement of objectives is salient, starting with the easier ones and then gradually moving to those being increasingly more complex. Pupils are tested at intervals to ascertain progress in objectives attainment. Testing provides results to the teacher in terms of what pupils missed or failed to understand. Computer printouts are available for teachers to assist in determining which test items were missed and remediation procedures may then be necessary.

Conclusion

Sequence is very important in pupil learning whether it be teacher determined or pupils with teacher guidance deciding upon the order of learning opportunities, each within the framework of the unit being emphasized. Perhaps, a combination of procedures may be utilized incorporating selected ideas from the following:

- Herbart's preparation, presentation, association, generalization, and use.
- Burner's spiral curriculum with revisits.
- Kilpatrick's project method and constructivism.
- Bagley with stress placed upon the basics in the curriculum.
- Behaviourism with its precise, measurably stated objectives and standardized testing to reveal pupil progress (Ediger, 2011).

REFERENCES

Ediger, Marlow (2011), "Meaning in the Social Studies," College Student Journal, 45 (2), 233-237.

Ediger, Marlow, and D. Bhaskara Rao (2003), Philosophy and Curriculum. New Delhi, India: Discovery Publishing House.

Wahlquist, John T. (1942), Philosophy of American Education. New York: Ronald Press Company.

CHAPTER 4

Curriculum Development and Attitudes in School Setting

Developing The Curriculum Takes Much Time And Effort When Emphasizing Quality In Teaching And Learning Situations. The pupil is the focal point of instruction and needs to experience a broad range of learning opportunities in the 21st century. More is expected of individuals, than ever before, in a complex world of technology and innovations. Relevant subject matter objectives are poignant to achieve in the diverse academic disciplines. Skill achievement stresses the importance of utilization of vital content acquired in different situations in life. The third kind of objectives to stress are attitudinal or affective objectives. This paper will focus on the latter of these three kinds of objectives in the curriculum.

The Attitudinal Objective in Instructional Arena

Too frequently, one hears of pupils having negative attitudes toward learning. This is exemplified in the following expressions:

- I never have liked school and will be glad to get out of here.
- I have never liked mathematics and do not do well here. My father hated math also.
- I do not like to learn from books, but desire to work with my hands.
- I will be glad to get a job after graduation so I will not have to go to school.

By viewing the above named statements, it appears that good attitudes toward schooling are lacking. Attitudinal objectives need identification and implemented in the school setting. These deal with the emotions of people and might well be very costly if left unattended. Individuals lose jobs at the work place due to poor attitudes; it may not be due to know how and skills possessed. Losing one's temper and/or telling the boss off are frequent causes for dismissal. Thus, the involved person must learn to regulate and govern the inherent feelings toward oneself as well as toward others. To be sure, not everything that happens will be acceptable. Individuals have their likes and dislikes in life; however, the problem remains that proper attitudes need to be adjusted to the involved situation. Situations differ one from the other, and feelings will be more intense in selected situations as compared to others. Thus, disappointments in life come and go and must be accepted, regardless of the fairness of the happening even though the teacher stresses the significance of justice in the classroom. The involved person needs to try to work out the problem. In problem solving, the problem is identified and hypotheses formed as possible solutions. Each hypothesis needs testing in a realistic situation to see if the consequences (solutions) are workable. Diverse solutions must be tried or hypotheses need changing in a flexible situation.

Too frequently, measurement specialists and educators, in general, believe that a standardized test is needed in administration to ascertain accurate information in the attitudinal dimension of pupil behaviour. To be sure, a reputable test might well shed light on the attitudes of learners. However, a classroom teacher who is knowledgeable may do a good job of assessing the attitudinal dimension. This is a person who is on the scene and interacts with pupils on a daily basis. Thus, the teacher notices how pupils work within functional committees in problem solving activities. Evaluation of the committee includes how well the involved pupil and ideas presented were respected. Creative thoughts which emphasize uniqueness, originality, and novelty are salient. Being able to take turns in presenting content orally and not interrupting aids in moving forward in a discussion. Thus, quality sequence and not jumping to unrelated ideas is poignant. Assisting others in the committee is relevant when it is necessary in respectful behaviour. There are numerous incidences which may be observed by the classroom teacher in advancing good attitudes (Ediger and Rao, 2014).

When supervising university student teachers in the public schools, the cooperating teacher told the writer quietly to observe two boys who were getting their jackets on to go outdoors for recess and how one of the two would be in tears shortly. This happened! The cooperating teacher had no idea as to what to do to remedy the situation. Possible solutions were discussed pertaining to this problem, including the separation of the two. It appears that schools need to identify these kinds of problems and have discussions pertaining there to. Different possible solutions need to be tried out in the classroom and school setting. It is good to iron out the difficulties so that interaction among all occurs and an increased democratic classroom evolves. Quality attitudes then have a good opportunity of surviving.

Learning Opportunities in the Classroom

The reading curriculum may certainly stress the attitudinal or affective dimension of instruction. Learners need to be able to choose their very own reading materials, from among others, in a selection. Thus, personalized reading might well be stressed. The library books available to pupils need to be sorted in terms of genera, such as animal stories, children of other lands, topical such as history, among others. The library books may also be sorted in terms of different reading levels. Methods of sorting need to accommodate learner interests and be convenient in checking in and out. The goal is to encourage good reading habits and interests. The teacher may briefly introduce a few books to children each day in an enthusiastic manner to whet appetites for reading. In personalized reading, the child is matched with suitable, fascinating reading materials. During this time devoted to silent reading, the teacher observes how interested the child is in reading. Words are pronounced as needed for the unidentified by selected children and the teacher.

If a pupil is not able to settle down with an interesting library book, the teacher may assist in making a choice. He/she knows children's literature well as well as the interest and reading level of the involved learner. Personalized reading should be an enjoyable time to concentrate, appreciate, and share that which has been read. Periodically, the teacher and a pupil need to have a conference to have the latter reveal comprehension with relevant questions to be answered in a non-threatening environment. The pupil might also read aloud a short selection to indicate fluency in reading content. With excitement and enthusiasm being stressed, the total conference might well be looked forward to by the learner as an enjoyable time of interaction with the teacher on a one on one basis. The teacher's time belongs to the pupil in this case.

Collaboration among pupils is poignant. They need to have opportunities to work together with others in the classroom setting. Members in collaboration should be those who are able to work together well; later on as collaboration succeeds, pupil with unlike social skills might well tackle a problem to solve as in mathematics. The emphasis is always upon pupils respecting each other and their ideas. Learning becomes increasingly favorable as the environment improves and learners are able to focus upon learning and not being ridiculed. Mathematics, also, lends itself well to having pupils work collaboratively in solving sequential problems, including those from a reputable mathematical textbook. Generally, as processes for learning are supportive and positive, pupils contribute more fully in the ongoing task. Creative and critical thinking skills are emphasized in problem solving in mathematics. The teacher's task is to assist learners to be fully engaged when collaborating with others. He/she may model orally whereby problem solving is involved in mathematics. Pupils need to understand and comprehend subject matter and utilize acquired knowledge to determine solutions. Satisfaction and joy are inherent in finding solutions when learning from each other. Focusing upon the problem and what it entails provide effort in achievement in working together on worthwhile subject matter. In a friendly atmosphere, pupils might well challenge each other in the ongoing problem solving activity. Learning is a social situation and invokes the use of relevant subject matter.

Pupil/teacher planning is important to emphasize. Planning involves decision making by those involved. The social studies, among other academic disciplines might well involve pupil/teacher planning of objectives to achieve a desired outcome. For instance, if pupils are studying a unit on The Middle Ages, with teacher guidance, they may decide to divide into committees to construct a manor, a tournament, a monastery, and a guild of workers. With approximately four to five on each committee, readiness for the endeavour may include the following:

- viewing a DVD on the Middle Ages, as well as looking at and discussing illustrations on a bulletin board showing different facts of life during that period of time.
- reading selections on the internet and selected library books on Medieval times.
- using the basal textbook as a point of departure for developing the construction project.

Committee members might also search for additional information as the Middle Ages project moves forward. The teacher's role is to guide pupils in keeping on track until the project has been completed. Each pupil needs to do his/her share and maintain responsibility in task completion. Assisting others, as needed in an atmosphere of respect, is a major objective to stress. Committees individually should report progress on the ensuing project to others. Leadership may emerge within a committee with no designated leader chosen. Pupils within each committee may move forward on their own with teacher encouragement and assistance.

Materials needed for the Medieval project should be conveniently available. Pupils need to share and keep materials, neatly, in their proper place. These might be kept within a committee while those materials for the common good being at a central supply center.

A rather unique approach in teaching a science unit observed by the writer when supervising university students in the public school setting emphasized a study of famous scientists in society. This stressed a biographical unit of study whereby pupils in committees chose a well known scientist in reporting the findings to classmate. Uniqueness and creativity was emphasized in presenting findings in report and/or display procedure. A listing was discussed within the class as a whole, with additional desired choices, flexibly approved by the teacher. The following choices were presented and made by learners:

- William Gilbert and his work and findings in magnetism.
- Galileo and has experiments pertaining to gravity from the leaning tower of Pisa.
- Sir Isaac Newton and his established laws of motion.
- Gregor Mendel and his experimentation involving the laws of heredity.
- Volta and his work with electrical batteries.

Committees were formed with three members per committee. The teacher reiterated rules to follow in having high quality committee work. The cooperating teacher and the student teacher role played a model whereby a participant would not interrupt other committee members in the presentation of ideas such as not digressing from the topic at hand.

Participants decided on how to present their findings to the others in the class setting. An outline, in proper form, of subject matter accompanied the project. For the project on magnets (see Gilbert above), the committee had a display of objects attracted to and repelled by horseshoe and bar magnets. The display had sequential illustrations, obtained from the internet, on scientists who did well in the field of inventions and their uses such as in electric motors, generators/alternators, and lifts to work in removing trash and other materials. It was indeed a fascinating topic to cover with learners being amazed at all the uses made of magnets and magnetism! Pupils from other classrooms came in to view and discuss each illustration and item. This project, along with others, was presented at a Parent/Teacher Association meeting. Favourable comments were heard and expressed by many (Ediger, 2010).

REFERENCES

Ediger, Marlow (2010), "Quality in the Mathematics Curriculum," Experiments in Education, 38 (2), 37-40.

Ediger, Marlow, and D. Bhaskara Rao (2014), School and Subjects, Issues and Concerns. New Delhi, India: Discovery Publishing House.

CHAPTER 5

Supervision and Morale in Curriculum

Each Curriculum Area Needs to Be Kept Updated

This means that continuous improvement in objectives, learning experiences, and evaluation techniques must be sought to provide the best educational experiences possible for pupils. At the same time, there must be adequate stability so that teachers can depend upon feelings of security and feelings of acceptance. Frequently, the two opposites are being emphasized with excessive change in too short a period of time as well as built in conservatism which advocates "sameness." Thus, innovations need to be sought after which will assist pupils to attain more optimally as well as maintaining that which is useful and enduring. Within that framework, school morale needs to be adhered to as being useful to accommodate teachers in fulfilling their respective roles in the curriculum.

Teacher morale is a salient feature in promoting excellence in schools. School morale is definitely related too changes as well as stability in the curriculum. Thus, a healthy school environment must be in the offing, beneficial to pupils, teachers, and school administrators. This is a difficult undertaking which must be sought enthusiastically by all those involved in the educational enterprise, parents included!

Building Morale and the Curriculum

How can schools work in the direction of building strong morale in an environment of change? Changes in the curriculum might bring on feelings of tension and anxiety in an otherwise secure environment. To be sure, the usual feelings of tension and anxiety may motivate an individual; however, excesses carry their weight. With an innovative curriculum being introduced, school leaders/supervisors need to follow selected tenets of change, which include the following:

- the ensuing curriculum must be understood and be meaningful to teachers. There needs to be adequate time for questions by teachers to clarify misunderstandings and vagueness.
- selected materials of instruction are at the meeting site and are available for comments and queries. Opportunities for perusing have been available previously, and now the materials to be utilized as learning activities provide examples for more indepth discussions.
- fears are allayed and minimized with the gradual induction of the new curriculum.
- the new curriculum is presented as opportunities and challenges, rather than force in making changes. A spirit of optimism must resonate among participants. Enthusiasm on the part of the supervisor might well reflect within participants (Ediger, 2013).

Second, trust is an important concept to stress, and this is built up over a period of time. Too frequently, mistrust is there which definitely hinders communication, and teachers might then wonder what the supervisor is attempting to pull on the participants. Mistrust, too, is detrimental in all dealings among faculty and staff in the school setting. Failure to relate honestly and effectively certainly hinder the trust equation. Thus, building trust must be ongoing and sequential, and not left to chance. A school is a social situation with many professionals and assistants; high quality communication is necessary to take care of curriculum and business needs. Trust involves good attitudes toward each other as well as effective communication skills. Relating well to others stresses good human relations. Self efficacy of teachers and supervisors improve within a trusting relationship. Very frequently, the knowledge base of school personnel increase with trust; reading, then as one avenue, to become better teachers and supervisors is an end result. The local school needs to possess a professional library consisting of university level textbooks a well as educational journals dealing with teaching the different academic and curriculum areas in the public schools. Time needs to be given with supervisor leadership in discussing recent literature read in the academic/curriculum areas. Implemented ideas from these readings should also be discussed and elaborated upon to encourage innovation of quality ideas.

Third, The affective dimension of teaching and learning should receive adequate attention in curriculum improvement endeavours. One of my university graduate students mentioned in class that no one took any particular notice of him or other teachers in his former school setting. He felt unimportant and minimized, leaving teaching after four years. Working for a roofing company as an office worker, he felt even less valued. The company failed to meet payroll deadlines and ultimately paid them every two months. The environment was uncouth and very unfriendly. He left this job and applied as a classroom teacher in the same school, learning that employed individuals need to pay attention to contributions made by employees. Bill, the graduate student, had barely gotten in again to the same school, having made plans at a local community college to major in computer software. It just so happened that three days before the new school your began, he received notice of school employment replacing a teacher who had moved to another state! Having realized that the school had not been as impersonal as previously thought, Bill sought a new times and places to recognize other teachers with enthusiastic greetings in the morning and taking note of an expressing judicial praise for good bulletin board displays, as well as other quality features of instruction. This resonated in developing a more wholesome school environment (Ediger, 2014).

Fourth, a school culture needs to exist which encourages a wholesome environment conducive to learning. Interest in achievement is salient for all in the school setting, teachers included. Thus, the school supervisor must desire to have an open cognitive environment which encourages questions and answers. If pupils are to be inquisitive, teachers and supervisors must be models to encourage critical and creative thinking, as well as problem solving. Pupils need encouragement to identify problems and work toward their solutions; school employees also need to ascertain problematic situations and work toward answers.

Culture stresses the values, beliefs, and ideals of a societal group or subgroup. Thus, a school may develop and build its very own culture which is conducive to learning and progress. Identifying problems in pupil learning requiring solutions emphasizes a continual stress upon the achievement of objectives. Inservice education also emphasizes the identification of difficulty in teaching and learning whereby teachers develop feelings of self efficacy. Confidence in the self results whereby the individual feels capable of assisting learner attainment, even in complex instructional situations. A developing school culture then:

- resonates with growth and accomplishment.
- respects all involved in those who are working collaboratively to offer the best curriculum possible.
- invites a feeling of belonging to a group to all members.
- emphasizes meeting esteem needs of each person, participants possessing worth and accomplishments.
- stresses assistance toward others in realizing more optimal achievement.

Effort is an important concept to emphasize in teaching and learning. Teachers must put forth much effort in planning the curriculum for pupils in the classroom; supervisors need to put forth considerable energy in staying abreast of salient trends in education as well as motivating inservice education endeavours. The following are salient for classroom teachers:

- assist each pupil to achieve as optimally as possible. This is a daunting task when there are 25-30 in a room, as well as when a few resist achieving objectives of instruction.

- work with all parents in collaborative endeavours to assist pupil learning. This can truly be difficult when selected parents are very verbal as well as being uncooperative.
- converse frequently with other teachers in cooperatively solving instructional problems.
- attempt to develop a friendly learning environment, conducive to cooperation in solving behavioral problems.

Supervisors have definite criteria to following:

- being patient with teachers in working toward curricular improvement within the framework of inservice education.
- visiting with teachers informally when introducing innovative ideas in teaching, as well as in group endeavours. Emphasize a school culture of teaching and learning; time for humor makes for relaxation and might well minimize stressful moments.
- stressing resilience assists teachers in recouping from moments of failure and is vital in curricular endeavours.

Conclusion

High quality moral is needed in all schools. The feeling dimension or affective domain is involved. Satisfying relationships for teachers, supervisors, pupils, and parents is necessary!

REFERENCES

Ediger, Marlow (2014), "Assisting Pupils in Learning," Research and Pedagogic Interventions, 3 (1), 9-15.

Ediger, Marlow (2013), "Teacher Observation to Evaluate Achievement," Delta K, 51 (10), 4-6.

CHAPTER 6

School Administrator, Morale and Curriculum

Good morale is at the the heart of teaching well in the school setting. Teachers have resigned or retired from teaching due to morale problems; it is difficult to come to school on any school day due to a poor environment to educate pupils properly. Rudeness, negative gossiping, putdowns, as well as talking back too frequently enter the workplace. A short term as well as longer engaged plans must be in the offing to improve the school climate, which in addition to boosting morale, should also aid pupil achievement. Pupils, teachers, and school administrators need a wholesome school environment to attain as optimally as possible. All are poignant in curriculum improvement endeavours.

Morale and the Curriculum

It is salient for pupils, teachers, and school administrators desiring to tackle the problems of the day in teaching and learning situations. Zest and motivation are in evidence in the school setting in assisting each individual to make sequential progress. When meeting for each new school day, teachers and principals need to greet each other with a wholesome, "Good morning!" It is the beginning of the day for new opportunities to help, assist, and motivate in an atmosphere conducive to learning. For example, the writer looks for new addresses to send manuscripts for publication in educational journals, every day. There are indeed very few places to send educational manuscripts to national journals in the United States. I find they refuse manuscripts as soon as they reach their offices. I do want to write and publish so I, instead, send articles for publication to state and foreign journals. Having gotten approximately two thousand published, I look for new opportunities for publication and do find them, this includes university level textbooks. Are these manuscripts inferior? This is for readers of subject matter to adjudicate. Nationally for educational journals, research articles are published and by/from the same writers/universities. Sometimes, selected people are chosen to write for United States national journals. I am 86 years old (Born 10-10-27) and still write every day with word processor use. By seeking new opportunities, and they are there, an increased energy level for life and living accrue. Life is worth living, even with a walker to get around as well as a helpful wife, I eagerly wait for a message of acceptance of a manuscript!

In the school setting, opportunities abound for salient roles and responsibilities. Mary Ediger, my wife and retired public school teacher, organized primary grade teachers with principal approval to discuss problems and progress of teaching primary grade pupils. Once involved teachers enjoyed the camaraderie, they infused topics to improve the curriculum. The comments were very positive from these meetings! There needs to be hope as a factor in motivating morale. At Truman State University, a new Division of Education head had a conference with each faculty member in the Division, and asked this question, among others, "What would make you happy while working in the Division of Education?" He explored answers in depth. This is quite different than, "You will do well because of receiving a monthly pay check," attitude. Time must be given to exploring dreams and visions which faculty members possess. These might well harmonize with improving the quality of instruction for graduate and undergraduate university students. In my situation, reading, surveying, and analyzing professional literature, contributed to offering the latest in innovations in the curriculum; writing for professional journals, then, can make for an updated curriculum.

There are a plethora of opportunities which assist in providing for esteem needs of faculty members in a school which include the following:

- serving as chairman of a faculty meeting. This should increase social skills as well as attempts being made to increase personal knowledge about curriculum development.
- taking a leadership role within the framework of inservice education.
- being a leader in trying out innovative teaching methodology, utilizing talents of members. Evaluation of the performance needs to be in the offing.
- supervisors commenting orally or in writing about the high qualities of teaching being revealed by a teacher.
- helping in planning a teacher/supervisor recognition dinner.
- working collaboratively to plan a holiday celebration.
- developing, within a committee setting, certificates of appreciation to be awarded to teachers.
- assisting in doing special events for pupils in recognition of achievement including good attitudes, among others.

Inservice education opportunities might well provide opportunities for selection of curriculum areas to focus upon in self assessment and improvement. There are selected concepts which need attention and may well provide for optimism. Resilience is poignant in school and in society. How many times do individuals experience failure and yet fail to realize the need to "bounce back" after experiencing the lack of minor/major successes? Problems experienced need to be looked upon as opportunities to learn and grow. Problems need identification and solutions sought. The consequences, herein, provide opportunities to achieve as well as acquire information and skills. Solutions need to be tried out within the involved situation. Risk taking is inherent in doing the solution. Collaboration is salient if trust is the culture of the school. Problems might well pertain to the following:

- discipline and behavioural incidences.

- getting selected pupils to learn and attain objectives of instruction.
- using motivational strategies in teaching.
- rewarding good behaviour in the classroom.
- implementing certain aspects of a new curriculum.
- working with hostile parents (Ediger, 2013).

Good morale is incremental when problems are solved. Trusting relationships are difficult to form and easy to break, but continual efforts must be made to work harmoniously with others. Trust as a concept when implemented makes for a more pleasant working environment. The work of a school is pleasant when people can rely upon each other. Teaching and learning are greatly hindered when:

- **Shunning individuals is in evidence:** One of my university colleagues resigned after six years on the job due to his Division Head not speaking to him. The Head of his Division would walk past the colleagues office and leave messages for him in his mail box. The colleague could not emotionally accept this kind of behaviour. Situations like these not only affect communication and trust, but also upon resigning his position, the selling of a home, the moving of the family, and his two boys not wanting to move due to friends made at the present school.
- **Certain people are marginalized:** Selected faculty members then are not in the "in-group." They feel neglected, unworthy, with unused talents. A great desire is being omitted here in that people want to be included in decision-making. Feelings of belonging are then being thrown under the bus. The writer volunteered for two years of service as a teacher and relief worker in the nation of Jordan, 1952-1954 with the Mennonite Central Committee (MCC). He whitewashed caves and homes of Palestinian Arab Refugees in Bethany, taught in the Mennonite School in Jericho and assisted in distributing

clothing in the Aqaba Jabber Refugee Camp directly south of the school. These scenes were eye opening and truly helped in my development with feelings of empathy. The writer ended his two years of service by teaching at Friends Boys School, a boarding school, located in Ramallah, ten kilometers north of Jerusalem. After returning to the home community in the United States, he felt increased inclusiveness by being asked to serve on many church and committees in the community with increased responsibilities due to having done relief work and teaching in the Holy Land, of all places! Service to humanity in diverse ways is salient for an individual to develop well socially as well as emotionally.

It behooves supervisors and teachers to notice who is not accepted and to help individuals become integrated into the school setting. A survey might well be completed whereby respondents indicate which committees and tasks they would like to participate in, the goal being to utilize the talents of all in the school setting.

Third esteem and recognition needs must be met. Upon teaching graduate and undergraduate university students, as well as speaking informally with them, the writer was amazed at talents revealed such as performing publicly in vocal or instrumental groups, writing and having published poetry, having traveled to unique areas of the world, among others. These need to be recognized and, if feasible, become an inherent part of the curriculum. When supervising university student teachers in the public schools, the following were brought into lessons and units taught:

- singing a native song with self accompaniment of a ukelele. This student was from Samoa.
- bringing into the classroom a trumpet to integrate its sounds of pitch and stress with a related science unit of study.
- having pupils view bedouin, nomadic costumes in sequential lessons on the Middle East in the social studies.

The university supervisor of student teaching, as well as teachers in the public schools should also contribute to ongoing lessons and units of study. The writer then showed slides of the Dome of the Rock, a Muslim octagonal mosque built in 619 AD; the Western Wall of the ancient Jewish synagogue; and the Church of the Holy Sepulcher; all located inside the walls of old Jerusalem. Each academic area should be made as concrete as possible for meaningful learnings to accrue. The abstract, consisting of printed script, generally, is the easiest to secure as teaching materials which include basal textbooks, internet sources, daily newspapers and newsmagazines, among others. Each pupil needs to understand how concrete materials are utilized within a culture or society, as well as the abstract in achieving objectives of instruction. When pupils experience meaning in the curriculum, they tend to like school better and possess higher morale as compared to rote learning and drill activities. Morale experiences emphasize teachers and supervisors trying out new learning activities; sameness dampens curiosity and interest (Ediger, and Rao, 2014).

REFERENCES

Ediger, Marlow (2013), "Issues in the Curriculum/'Research and Pedagogic Interventions, 2(2), 9-13.

Ediger, Marlow, and d. Bhaskara RAo (2014), School Subjects, Issues and Concerns. New Delhi, India: Discovery Publishing House.

CHAPTER 7

Curricular Ideas from Great Leaders of the Past

A study of the history of education provides information on poignant educational leaders of the past. These educators provided foundational ideas for teachers and school administrators to utilize and build upon. The ideas also provide a structure for educational practices in everyday instruction, with additions and modifications to be made. Then to, a study of the history of education provides insight into practices of the past and why innovations were necessary. Selected educators will be discussed in the contents.

Problems in the Curriculum

Michael of Montaigne, Renaissance educator (1533 - 1582), advocated the use of excursions in teaching pupils. Schools in his day were cruel places of physical punishment and he realized that individuals learned much when living in the natural and social environment. Michael of Montaigne believed that pupils would learn much more and in a pleasant way by visiting people from different cultures. Adults would be there to supervise pupils in these traveling situations.

Excursions are still recognized by educators as being salient. They do take time to make arrangements, including safety needs of pupils. Modern technology has made it possible to bring into the classroom AV materials which substitute or add to actual excursions to a place of interest, including the following:

- video tapes and DVDs which are of high quality and assist pupils in observing realistic scenes and sights. A carefully chosen video on the Middle Ages presents scenes with peripherals on lords and manors, knights on horse back and tournaments for spectators to see, as well as guild workers working on different tasks. Extended learnings might be provided through projects and research activities.

- a lay person coming into the classroom to demonstrate making butter or other food product. The resource person specializes in a certain topic or facet of knowledge and skills.
- a mime or person who specializes in dramatic activities which brings history to life for learners.
- a person who has much knowledge due to living in and/ or traveling to a foreign nation being studied. Visuals of high quality are always welcome in these situations (Ediger and Rao, 2012).

Teachers need to be on the lookout for talent within a community to assist in enriching experiences for learners. There are Educators from nearby colleges who might be willing to come to speak on a historical figure and at the same time utilize AV aids. Resource people must have high quality communicative talents in connecting with younger people.

A second Educator who changed teaching and learning situations much was Friedrich Wilhelm Pestalozzi (1746 - 1827). Instead of dull, uninspiring lectures, Pestalozzi advocated the use of object lessons. Here, pupils could visualize a concrete situation relating to the abstract. Thus in studying an insect such as a grasshopper, pupils could see first hand the head, thorax, and abdomen. The feelers on the head might also be pointed out to pupils. This provided readiness for a discussion on the purposes of each body part as well as for reading about grasshoppers. The concrete phase of learning is usually the easiest for pupils and assists in meaningful learning in discussions and in reading related subject matter.

Pestalozzi believed in school settings to be joyous places of learning. Instead of physical punishment of children for not meeting teacher expectations in achievement, schools were to be inviting and places of encouragement. There was even singing by pupils in the hallways of the school structure.

A third leading Educator who changed teaching and learning situations was Johann Friedrich Herbart (1776 - 1841). Herbart developed his own teacher training schools in which he paid attention to sequence in pupil learning. He is known for developing the lesson plan which contained ordered steps to be followed by teachers in teaching pupils. In his subject centered curriculum, Herbart stressed the following sequence:

- **Preparation:** This consisted of review of salient parts of the previous lesson so that readiness for the ensuing would resonate. Too frequently, in his day, lessons were disconnected from each other.
- **Presentation:** The new subject matter was presented to pupils, by relating it to the step of preparation.
- **Association:** Here, learners were aided to make associations of the new and the previously taught subject matter. Content was not to be held in abeyance in isolation. But rather, relationships were gleaned which then would be remembered for a longer period of time. Herbart stressed the importance of history and literature in planned lessons. However, his planned approach would work equally well in relating other academic areas.
- **Generalization:** Pupils need to develop conclusions and summaries of what has been learned; otherwise, a hedge podge of unrelated facts might not make sense nor survive in the minds of learners.
- **Use:** Pupils need to utilize that which was learned, otherwise relevancy in learning wold be minimized as well as forgetting occurred.

A fourth Educator in history to have much influence in the curriculum was Friedrich Froebel. He is considered as a being a pioneer in kindergarten education. Young children were attracted to Froebel who was strong in stressing *creative* endeavours for learners. His emphasis upon pupils being in a circle and then dramatizing creatively what was being sung stressed unique learning opportunities for young children in a day of rigidity and harsh methods of memorization which were the order of the times. Thus in singing about gardening, pupils might dramatize, in a creative manner—preparing the soil, planting seeds, hoeing the garden to take out weeds, as well as picking flowers/fruit from the mature plants. In art work, originality of products produced emphasized by each pupil brought that which is within a child to the surface in art products and processes. Froebel's educational philosophy is noticed in the following present day classroom learning activities:

- originality rather than rote learning is stressed.
- uniqueness, novelty, as well as creativity is fostered.
- pupils liking the teacher, schooling, and education rather than fearing harsh approaches used in discipline and education in general.
- pupils are to be respected and cared for in school and in life.

A fifth Educator whose work is still very prevalent in schools today is William Heard Kilpatrick (1871 - 1964) and his project method. Dr. Kilpatrick noticed that the project method was used much in organizations for rural youth in his day. Thus, a child had, for example, a dairy project whereby the he/she would care for and keep record of expenses and profits which came form the project as well as take proper care of the livestock. Thus in the classroom and school environment, pupils also would work on projects, directly related to ongoing units of study. Social theory was being emphasized in that pupils worked collaboratively on a carefully identified project. Dr. Kilpatrick identified the following, broad, flexible steps in project development:

- there had to be a ***purpose*** in doing the project. Thus, reasons were there for participation in this activity. This was not determined by the teacher, but came about as a result of pupils choosing the project with teacher assistance. If pupils perceived a purpose in doing the project, motivation and energy were there to fulfill its ongoing. Pupil purpose was needed to accept relevancy in teaching and learning situations.

- meticulous ***planning*** of the purpose was necessary to do well in its success. Slovenly and careless work was to be avoided. Too frequently, pupils failed to plan carefully to achieve the desired end result.
- ***carrying out of the plans*** meant that each committee member creatively did his/her share of the entailed work. Cooperation was needed in collaborative endeavours.
- ***evaluating*** the finished project. Criteria were established to guide the evaluative process. These might well have included neatness, effort, working well together, and thoroughness (Ediger and Rao, 2003).

A sixth Educator, John Dewey (1859 - 1952), developed a laboratory school at the University of Michigan where he was then Professor of Philosophy in the later 1800s. The laboratory school emphasized integrating school and society. What is salient in society should also be important in school learnings. Problems exist in society and those selected might well become poignant for pupils to consider with the teacher being a guide and stimulator, but not a lecturer nor sage on the stage. Within a committee setting, pupils select a problem or problems which require deliberation in working toward a tentative solution. A child centered curriculum is in evidences since pupils identify and tentatively solve a problem. Dewey believed that knowledge is not an absolute, but subject to modification and change. Problem solving is important in school as well as in society. Once a problem has been carefully delineated, hypotheses are developed. Each hypothesis given by learners is subject to testing, in a life like manner. Hypotheses may be modified and revised as needed. A new problem might be selected as a result of the deliberation. Critical thinking is involved in separating the relevant from the irrelevant, fantasy from reality, and the significant from the insignificant.

Conclusion

Teachers, principals, and supervisors can benefit much by studying salient educators of the past who provided important ideas for present day consideration in teaching and learning. The ideas gleaned need some modification and change to be relevant in today's educational setting. Then too, a well educated educator should have a sound basis of knowledge and skills in being a well rounded person.

REFERENCES

Ediger, Marlow, and D. Bhaskara Rao (2012), Essays in Teaching the Social Studies. New Delhi, India: Discovery Publishing House.

Ediger, Marlow, and D. Bhaskara Rao (2003), Philosophy and Curriculum. New Delhi, India: Discovery Publishing House.

CHAPTER 8

Philosophy as an Academic Area of Study in Schools

Philosophy as a liberal arts academic discipline might be taught as a separate subject or integrated into the social studies curriculum. There are a plethora of philosophers which are relevant for pupil study; thus a careful study needs to be made as to which are most relevant for public school pupils. The author will elaborate on a few, but there are numerous others which deserve attention (Ediger and Rao, 2010).

Philosophy in the Curriculum

Plato (427 - 422 BC) of ancient Greece is a very familiar name in philosophical endeavours. In his classical book titled, The Republic. Plato emphasized three categories of workers in his changeless ideal nation. Rulers who governed the nation were at the apex. They would receive the most schooling and were sorted out to become leaders in the the ideal Republic as governmental officials. The second highest official in Plato's Republic were the Warriors. They served the nation in keeping out enemies from within and outside the borders of the ideal state. The third and last category in the Republic were the workers. They provided the necessary goods and services for citizens.

Discussions of the three categories of workers might well center around the following topics, among others:

- How have the categories changed in number and work performed by each when making comparisons with the present day?
- How is the level of education presently used to fulfill jobs and professions similar to Plato's thinking and how is it different?

- How is change in society perceived presently with that of the ideal Republic of Plato?

Aristotle (384 - 322 BC) has had great influence in education, past and present. Aristotle's philosophy of education contains many beliefs, therein, as emphasized by the medieval philosopher ST. Thomas Acquinas. Aristotle stressed causes for what transpired. In observing artisans of his day, he noticed the following in sequential occurrences:

- **Material cause:** Thus, there is physical matter which is used in diverse ways to construct objects and items, to engage in an activity. In Aristotle's day, for example, the sculptor used natural rock as a material cause.
- **Formal cause:** The sculptor designs the matter into a human figure. The form or shape then comes into being.
- **Efficient cause:** There is a doer in changing the material into a form or being.
- **Final cause:** This stresses the use(s) which will be made of the completed item(s), which in this case, is a statue of a revered individual.

Pupils with teacher guidance, using the above asterisked items of Aristotle, might be assisted to think of something representing matter, such as one or more newspapers which may be cut into one inch wide strips, approximately six inches long. These may be soaked in water within a basin. A mixture of flour is added to the soaked strips of paper (drain the water first) in the basin to make a medium paste. The paper strips are then massaged onto an empty roll of paper toweling. The paper is made smooth by working on it until the desired shape sin evidence. An animal, a head of a human, among others might well result by shaping and attaching to the soaked newspaper. Use tempera paint to complete making facial expressions, among others.

In the above example, the newspaper is the material cause while the shaping is the formal cause. The efficient cause is the pupil with teacher assistance. The final cause might stress the products be made for an exhibit in the classroom for others to view or for a parent/teacher conference. In Aristotle's day the final cause would be a statue made in honour of a famous person in ancient Greece. The project method may be utilized in any social studies, science, mathematics, or reading/language arts unit of study.

Michael of Montaign (1533 - 1582) of Renaissance times advocated travel as a means of educating children. He opposed the type of cruelty which existed in schools of his day; physical punishment was then utilized to "motivate" learning. Michael of Montaign was interested in humane ways of educating pupils through travel. Here, pupils would learn about the history, geography, and culture of diverse groups in society. Adequate supervision would be available to develop and maintain safety for learners. Thus, children might learn from first hand, direct experiences. Reality is brought into the curriculum. This procedure might well be related to excursions and field trips within ongoing units of study. Excursions are very important in today's curriculum and can be as easy to implement as having pupils in a science unit notice evaporation of water occurring on the local school grounds when noticing a puddle of water becoming dry on a day to day basis. With the many AV aids, as well as illustrations available, pupils with readiness might observe a video/illustration pertaining to what transpires in the community and this could pertain to science, social studies, reading and literature, as well as mathematics.

A fourth philosopher to study is Ralph Waldo Emerson (1803 - 1882). Emerson was an optimist who lived at a time when the frontier areas were wide and open. There were a plethora of opportunities available to seek one's own fortune in a variety of kinds of work endeavours. In spite of illnesses within his own family such as his father dying in Emerson's youth, his brother dying at a young age, and his wife dying in the early years of marriage, Ralph Waldo Emerson remained an optimist in future endeavours. Resilience appears to be a clear factor in his life with abilities to bounce back from unfortunate situations. Beyond resilience being a marvelous trait to possess, Emerson emphasized the following:

- **Trusting in one's own thinking:** There are, of course, people who do not function well due to a lack of confidence.
- **Leaning upon the self for decision-making:** Too many people lean upon other's decisions which do not fit the situation involving problem solving.
- **Conforming and conformity are the hob goblins of little men:** Creative thinking brings on fresh, new ideas which might well benefit the self and society.

Resilience and creativity are two vital concepts for children to develop in daily living. Failure should not be an option and creative solutions to problems are needed to lift the self into feelings of success. This requires the ability to lean upon the self and make fewer excuses for failures, be they minor or major. Teachers, here, may discuss with pupils the following:

- how might you be helped to minimize failures and optimize new opportunities to bounce back from unpleasant experiences?
- how might successes, and less of failure, be emphasized more for each pupil in ongoing learning activities?
- why do individuals depend upon others to do their thinking when meeting up with a dilemma?

A fifth philosopher who contributed much to emphasize what is relevant in the curriculum is John Dewey (1859 - 1952), late professor of philosophy at Columbia University. He had his own laboratory school for pupils which stressed an activity centered curriculum. Here, pupils would "learn by doing," with a hands on approach in learning. Rote learning, mental discipline, and memorization of subject matter were eliminated. Dewey emphasized the concept of change in everyday living. Absolutes do not exist, but changes occur in time and place. Since changes occur due to innovations and technology, pupils with teacher assistance need to become proficient in problem solving. New problems arise and old solutions might not fit in as possible solutions. Solutions are tentative and subject to change. In ongoing units of study then, Dewey recommended that pupils identify a problem or problems. In collaborative settings, pupils suggest an hypothesis to the problem. Each hypothesis is recorded for all to see in the small group. They are then grouped into categories to avoid duplication or omissions. Agreed upon hypotheses are tested in an activity centered curriculum. Deliberation and time is involved in coming up with a supported hypothesis. Along the way, the problem may need to be changed or modified. It might be, too, that a completely new problem is accepted for possible solution. After testing the hypotheses, revisions may need to be made as revealed in the collaborative discussion. Implications for Dr. Dewey's approach in present-day teaching and learning involve the following:

- pupils should be encouraged and motivated to raise indepth questions pertaining to subject matter being studied.
- critical and creative thinking must be stressed in arriving at answers.
- knowledge acquired must be considered as being tentative and subject to possible change.
- social development is poignant in that pupils with teacher leadership work in small groups.

A sixth educational philosopher, salient for curriculum development consideration, is William Heard Kilpatrick (1871 - 1964). Dr. Kilpatrick emphasized the project method in teaching and learning situations. He brought his ideas on projects from farm organized clubs for pupils, such as 4H and FFA, to the public school classroom. Rote learning and memorization, definitely, were not stressed in ongoing units of study. Rather, pupils with teacher guidance would discuss and select a project within a committee setting. The chosen project possessed value to the participants whereby interest was inherently high. Kilpatrick used the term ***purpose*** on the part of learners in project selection. The purpose or reasons for project development came from pupils. Once the purpose was intrinsically accepted for doing the project, ***planning*** was involved. The plans were thoroughly discussed as to materials needed and who did what. Much leeway was left for creative thinking, in that pupils did their very own sequencing of ideas. The teacher assisted in keeping tasks sequential and ongoing. In Dr. Kilpatrick's flexible order, pupils engaged in carrying out the plans; here, the concept ***executing*** was utilized to show progress in doing the activity. Careful work was needed in carrying out the plans. Finally, the project needed to be evaluated which was called ***judging***. Criteria were developed by pupils with teacher guidance to appraise the completed project. Criteria might well include neatness, accuracy, effort put forth, among others (Ediger and Rao, 2003).

Conclusion

Pupils need to become familiar and utilize different schools of thought in reasoning and in problem solving. A study in philosophical schools of thought add to the dimensions of learners being able to focus upon thinking effectively in problem solving.

REFERENCES

Ediger, Marlow, and D. Bhaskara Rao (2011), Essays in Teaching the Social Studies. New Delhi, India: Discovery Publishing House.

Ediger, Marlow, and D. Bhaskara Rao (2003), Philosophy and Curriculum. New Delhi, India: Discovery Publishing House.

CHAPTER 9 Seat Time in an Informal Curriculum in the Classroom vs Learning to Achieve Predetermined Objectives

Much is written in educational literature and practices pertaining to seat time in an informal curriculum versus achieving predetermined, measurably stated objectives in ascertaining credits to be issued. The Carnegie Unit is traditional and is based upon, for example, pupils being in class fifty minutes each day, five days a week, and nine months in the school year. This permits time for instruction in an open ended manner in which pupils have more opportunities for making choices, among alternatives, and for decision-making. Selected educators believe that much time is wasted in this type of arrangement. They would advocate the use of precise, measurably stated objectives which can be checked off as each goals is attained. Continuous progress in meeting these goals is stressed in ongoing lessons and units of study.

An Open Ended Curriculum

Learning centers might well be one approach to be utilized here with an ample number of centers per room so that three to five pupils might work at each center. Generally, there are task cards at each center with four learning activities per card. The tasks are clearly written so they are understandable by learners. The tasks pinpoint one or more objectives of instruction. Thus, pupils may select which to work on and which to omit. Ensuing tasks might be written as the need arises. The tasks might well emphasize the following kinds or types (Ediger and Rao, 2012):

- strictly academic in nature, whereby pupils secure in problem solving, for example, on history, such as the causes of the French Revolution of 1789.

- collaborative endeavours whereby pupils choose to work in a committee to trace developments leading to the French Revolution.
- involvement in a seminar after taking a position/securing background information pertaining to the Tennis Court Oath of the French Revolution.

A second open ended approach in teaching and learning might well be for a student to select from among several listed alternative learning opportunities; he/she might then choose a minimal number to complete. Thus, for example if seven questions are listed the student may choose four to complete. The choice could also be to answer all questions. Definite standards would need to be met to perform satisfactorily on the minimal number with extra credit given for quality efforts on the remainder of the responses. Slovenly work is not acceptable; rubrics may be developed to assist in the assessing.

A third open ended approach emphasizes a debate between opposing sides. Was the French Revolution avoidable?" might be the heart of the debate. Much research would need to be done to participate in the debate in accepting the pro versus the con side of the debate to develop an indepth set of arguments. The debate could takeplace inside the classroom and require considerable research. Each side of the debate needs to pursue the research indepth to be highly knowledgeable. The rules for debating needs to receive ample consideration. A video tape played of a model debate with resulting discussions should be a prerequisite. The ensuing debate needs to be recorded and assessed in terms of criteria. Many pupils enjoy debating and it provides an enticing learning opportunity involving knowledge and skills. The writer in supervising university student teachers noticed a motivating effect in learning in achieving objectives of instruction using the debate method. It appeared as if energy levels for achieving were intrinsically high (Ediger, 2011). A few participating pupils asked to have another debate whereas listeners also wanted to be active participators.

The above are just three examples of an open ended curriculum. The advantages are the following:

- more autonomy for learning whereby choices and decision making are involved.
- subject matter to be acquired becomes interesting when there are challenges to learn.
- positive attitudes are displayed with choice of learning activities being involved.
- trust is being emphasized that pupils have rights in choosing from among alternatives.
- intrinsic motivation is stressed when pupils develop higher energy levels for attaining personal goals, based on their needs and wants.

Project methods, frequently, are stressed in an open curriculum. Here within a unit of study, pupils choose a project. Generally three to four pupils work on a project, but an individual might well select a worthwhile endeavour. The project is purposeful and has background reasons for its acceptance. It is based on what has been studied or learned previously and now is a challenge to an ensuing experience. The selected project is goal centered and might stress a hands on approach in learning, although projects may be abstract in nature consisting of academic knowledge. Once a project has been accepted as having much worth, pupils in a committee or individually, develop plans to achieve the purpose. Careful planning is necessary; however, pupils will pursue the specifics sequentially as in a constructivist philosophy of learning. Sequence, then, resides within the pupil in ongoing experiences.

The teacher's role, in using the project method of instruction, is being an advisor and offering assistance to learners as needed. The teacher is not a lecturer nor a sage on the stage, but a helper in a constructive manner as he/she circulates within and among committees, as well as assisting an individual to make progress. It takes a good supervisor to keep and maintain on task behaviour. Thus, all collaborative members need to contribute and develop appropriate sequence in the undertaking. A mistake is made when one or two of a committee do all the work in developing a project with the others being satisfied that somebody is completing the project. The actual doing part of the project entails high quality work to fruition.

In addition to perceiving a purpose, planning to achieve the purpose, as well as implementing the plans in an authentic activity, the final stage is appraisal. The teacher has continuously evaluated the committee's endeavours: however, pupils involved in the ***doing*** aspect must also appraise their own completed project. This is an important part of learning. Criteria need to be developed and may be utilized in all facets of the project's development and completion. Pupils with teacher leadership may then do the standards for evaluation. In observing pupils in the school setting when appraising university student teachers in action, the following criteria have generally been developed, among others:

- the quality of interaction among participants.
- neatness of the product in its finality.
- effort put forth by committee members.
- achievement of objectives when doing the project.
- creative behaviour exhibited by individuals.

Questions should be raised and problems identified by learners in the ongoing experience. Curiosity is an attitude which should permeate all learning. To reiterate, constructivism is a major philosophy in project methods learning in which learners tend to sequence their own progress within the confines of teacher assistance. This provides pupils with increased autonomy and freedom whereby they possess personal ownership of the ongoing activity.

Teaching Toward Measurably Stated Objectives

Precise objectives are preplanned, prior to their implementation in the classroom. The specific objectives may be mandated or developed within a school system. These kinds of ends leave little/no leeway for interpretation. Pupils know what is expected of them when viewing the stated objectives. The teacher, too, is clear on expectations from pupils as a result of teaching toward the precise ends of instruction. Then too, evaluation of pupil achievement, reflecting the objectives, may be known through knowledge and skills achieved as a result of instruction. The measurable stated objectives movement emphasize the following:

- precision in what exists, exists in some amount, and if it exists in some amount, it can be measured.
- the objectives, learning opportunities, and evaluation procedures are, interrelated and provide the basis for the measurable stated objectives movement.
- the basics or essentials are emphasized in the precise ends of instruction.
- efficiency of instruction is being emphasized with no time available for the peripheral or non-essentials.
- the focal point is on the objectives to be achieved; they are paramount and accomplished through the learning activities, selected by the teacher. Evaluation is to realize with certainty if the objectives have been achieved by pupils.
- pupil progress might then be compared with that of other learners in the classroom. School averages might well also be available in making comparisons.
- definite data is available to chart learner progress.

Measurability has its roots in programmed learning whereby the programmer determines the objectives for pupils to achieve. Either in book or computer form, the pupil responds to closely sequenced items in which the learner views an item, such as a few statements of subject matter to acquire and then answers a question pertaining to what was read. The answer is in the statement of content read prior to the completion test item which provides the correct answer with reinforcement involved in being correct most of the time. If the pupil responds correctly, he/she is ready for the next sequential bit of information to be read, followed by a question based on that content. If correct, the pupil moves forward to the next sequential bit of information to be read. If incorrect, the learner still moves forward to the next sequential item since the correct answer was observed. The sequence is the same throughout each program with read, respond to a test item, and then check the response.

There is also a branching programmed learning procedure which stresses when an incorrect response is given by a pupil, he/she reads ordered statements with opportunities to respond to each until the pupil rejoins where the incorrect answer was given. The pupil is then ready to proceed with the sequential items of programmed learning. As is true of numerous plans of teaching and learning, there are inherent weaknesses in utilizing behaviourally stated objectives and measurement procedures in instructional procedures in education:

- it is entirely predetermined if programs are written entirely by programers, leaving little/no leeway for pupil interaction. This is true too in non-programmed plans if teachers depend largely upon pupils achieving the measurably stated objectives written by academic specialists in their academic areas of specialty. The objectives are then highly precise and its either/or if learners attain each stated objective.
- it is weak in emphasizing attitudinal goals such as resiliency, effort put forth by learners, and motivation.
- it is rather rigid and formal in that only/largely measurability is stressed in teaching.
- it might become difficult for teachers to locate learning opportunities which harmonize with the stated objectives.
- it places too much emphasis upon evaluation, rather than the instructional process.

The Psychology of Learning

There are selected tenets from the psychology of learning which should permeate all facets of instruction. These vital components which assist all pupils to do well in learning include the following:

- pupil purpose or reasons for achieving.
- interest in learning involving active participation/ appropriate sequence in learning be it teacher and/or pupil determined.
- quality appraisal procedures which provide feedback for ensuing experiences.
- provision made for individual differences among pupils.
- use of proper grouping procedures.
- integration of needed technology to aid learner progress.

REFERENCES

Ediger, Marlow (2011), Collaborative versus Individual Endeavors in the Curriculum," Education, 132 (1), 217-220.

Ediger, Marlow, and D. Bhaskara Rao (2012), School Subjects, Issues and Concerns. New, Delhi, India, Discovery Publishing House.

CHAPTER 10

Standardized Tests and Curriculum

How often should pupils be tested when using standardized tests? There are schools in which teachers have refused to administer these tests due to their frequency of use in ascertaining learner achievement. Too be sure, it does take away a chunk of instructional time for each administration. There is a further problem in determining what pupils have accomplished, especially if the standardized tests are misaligned with teaching and learning situations.

This paper will focus upon possible excesses in the utilization of standardized tests.

Testing to Determine Pupil Progress

Standardized tests need to determine that which is relevant and salient for pupils to learn. Higher levels of thinking should be in evidence such as critical and creative thinking as well as problem solving. Rote learning and memorization need to be greatly minimized. It is relatively essay to write these kinds of items and they lend themselves to massive and quick machine scoring. However, there are complaints that standardized test results do not come back in time to be of value to the teacher and school administrator. Then too, there are a plethora of errors from machine scoring in selected school districts and states. As of this writing (March 15, 2014), the State of North Carolina has called a halt in releasing standardized test scores due to many glitches therein. High school seniors desiring their school grade point average and rank, along with test results, are not able to secure these data in time for college/university admission. A few other states have had errors in printouts whereby the lowest classroom performers received the highest scores and the higher obtaining the lower scores. Even one error per high school graduate's test results can indeed be very damaging. With mass testing, it certainly is possible to have glitches in computer scoring (Ediger and Rao, 2013).

An increased number of states are or are planning to track pupil progress, Kindergarten through grade twelve. The tracking generally is a plan of keeping track of a pupil's test scores, K-12, in relation to a selected annual standardized test. It could emphasize, too, anecdotal statements entered based on an observed pupil behaviour inside the classroom or on the school grounds, in addition to conduct outside the school setting. The anecdote might be highly unfavourable to a pupil; this remains on record for years to come and might hinder job securing and/or college/university admittance, even though behavioural changes are definitely possible. What is on the hard drive remains there for years to come.

What is the answer to the above named problems? There is a need for accurate and unbiased recordings of pupil achievement to notice sequential progress and yet this can be carried to a negative extreme. The following are suggested remedies:

- make certain that computerized scores are accurate.

  Teachers and school administrators need to evaluate these scores with comparisons made to classroom performance. The best measures possible should be utilized to ascertain learner progress.

- study different recommended standardized achievement tests to notice the validity and reliability of each as given in the Manual. A test needs to be valid to measure what a school desires to evaluate. Thus if knowledge and skills in division of fractions is emphasized in the school setting, the test should then measure these competencies. A high validity figure must be stressed in the manual of the standardized test. Reliability of a test emphasizes consistency of measurement for the standardize test being used or being considered. Thus, if test/retest reliability data is listed in the Manual, which it must or other approaches to reliability, then the figure provided should be high for a test to measure consistently. Alternative forms or split half reliability might also be given to indicate or specify reliability of the test.

- standardized tests should be given as directed in the Manual for test administration, otherwise the results from one's own pupils will not reflect the pupil's achievement in relationship to the norms of the test.

Printouts of test results for each classroom need to be available to notice which items were missed most frequently. This provides feedback to the teacher of learner achievement. He/she notices what needs reteaching and what was not taught in teaching and learning situations. If standardized tests are worthwhile in their administration, they should provide information as to which objectives need further emphasis.

To reiterate, teacher observation of pupil achievement also has much merit. Up to date criteria must be utilized. There is much to notice in learner behaviour which does affect academic achievement and test results. The following are salient:

- rudeness and negative remarks should be minimized or banned. It is hurtful if pupils intimidate, harass, and/ or inflict physical pain. Sarcasm and ill will have their penalties in hindering pupil progress.
- treat pupils and their ideas with respect.
- work toward having high quality human relations in school and in society.
- emphasize problem solving when working toward improved human relations. Behavioural problems need identification and solutions.

Teachers need to model good behaviour for pupils to emulate. This will positively affect test scores when a good learning environment is in evidence.

Intensive drill is to be frowned upon when having pupils developing readiness for taking a standardized test. There are public schools where this is done excessively. There are items of importance in developing readiness such as educating pupils on the mechanics of test taking including the format utilized therein. Again, valuable instructional time is lost when sessions are devoted to excessive rehashing of subject matter for testing. Then too, interest is lost in learning with the heavy use of drill (Ediger, 2010).

Conclusion

Instead of heavy use of drill in test taking, the writer recommends that teachers follow important principles of teaching and learning which include:

- securing and maintaining pupil interest in achievement of salient goals of instruction.
- assisting learners to perceive purpose or reasons for achieving what is relevant in school and in society.
- providing for individual differences so each pupil attains as optimally as possible.
- having pupils attaching meaning and understanding to subject matter acquired.
- helping pupils to put forth effort as well as being resilient.
- emphasizing social development among learners.

REFERENCES

Ediger, Marlow, and D. Bhaskara Rao (2013), Essays in Teaching Mathematics. New Delhi, India: Discovery Publishing House.

Ediger, Marlow (2010), Data Driven Decision Making in the Social Studies, Education, 131 (2), 359-362.

CHAPTER 11
Oral Communication, Pupil and Curriculum

Quality oral communication skills are needed by pupils to convey information in school and in society. Growth in these areas is ongoing and must receive adequate emphasis in all curriculum areas. Pupils need to interact with the thinking of others in class and in the school setting. There are different classifications of oral communication which need incorporation in daily lessons plans. Among others, these include the following:

- conversation with participants.
- persuasive speaking.
- presentation of oral reports.
- meeting and greeting others.
- discussions in small groups or in class as a whole.
- presiding at a meeting.
- being an officer of a club or organization.
- complimenting others for an achievement.

The above, among others, provide for rich experiences in oral use of language. These activities need to be planned carefully with carefully selected objectives. There must be balance among understandings, skills, and attitudinal objectives. The teacher needs to have high, reasonable expectations of each learner in attainment of objectives. Learning activities need to harmonize with the chosen ends and make provision for individual differences. Success for learners is salient and possess building blocks for future ensuing successful endeavors. Assessment provides information in terms of how well each pupil is achieving.

The Psychology of Learning and Oral Communication

The psychology of learning provides guidelines for teacher use in curriculum development. Each teacher must be mindful of these psychological principles in teaching and learning situations. This aids in providing for optimal learner progress in oral communication, as well as in other facets of curricular concerns. First of all, teachers need to be certain that pupil interest is fostered. For example, what would capture learner interest in a social studies unit on Egypt? Pupil choice is poignant, and perhaps, the great pyramids would provide fascinating information. Thus, a committee may choose this topic and select a project for their report. A variety of reference sources might be utilized including the internet. Within the committee, learners may discuss collaboratively how to secure necessary information. The teacher is a guide and stimulator. By using a carefully developed rubric, pupils might assist in appraising their own performance, along with that of the teacher.

Purpose must be involved in the oral communication learning activity. Thus, in selecting the Great Pyramids for a project, learners need to perceive that it is worthwhile. There are facts, concepts, and generalizations which they wish to attain. Through discussions as a learning activity, pupils zero in on specific values within the topic. Ensuing learnings accrue as the search for information is ongoing. Evaluation of the contents, too, occur within committee endeavors. Flexible rules need to be developed and followed in communicating orally and these include:

- maintaing focus upon the central idea and its relationship to subordinate subject matter.
- each committee member should contribute as optimally as possible.
- clarity in the presentation of ideas is important.
- creativity is to be encouraged.

Energy levels for learning increase as pupils increasingly perceive purpose in achievement. Time spent in having pupils perceive purposes in oral communication experiences is time well spent. In supervising university student teachers in the public schools, the writer noticed the enthusiasm shown by pupils in a project if they had a voice in determining and shaping its outcomes. The project then stresses the saliency of purpose, planning, carrying out its development, and then evaluation of its quality.

Second, motivation needs accentuating in teaching and learning situations. An ill prepared teacher, lecturing in a monotone voice will not cut it in ongoing lessons and units of study. Motivation assists in making for effort in the classroom. Thus, pupils need to feel the worth of an ongoing activity. In a project method, pertaining to the Middle East, pupils may be stimulated, via a video presentation, to develop a mural of the walled city of Jerusalem. Studying for and developing a mural provides pupils with subject matter knowledge, art experiences, as well as in persuasive oral communication skills. The wall around Jerusalem must be portrayed with inherent inside Holy structures. The Western Wall, also called the wailing wall, is the only remnant of the ancient Jewish Temple. Here, devout Jews gather to offer prayers directly in front of their holiest structure on earth. The earliest Temple was built in the days of King Solomon, approximately 1000 BC. Directly above and slightly east in a mountainous region is the Dome of the Rock, an octagonal mosque, from which devout Muslims worship and offer prayers, five times day. From this area, Mohammed ascended into heaven and returned to earth again, according to devout followers of Islam. Jerusalem is the third holiest city of Islam; Mecca, Saudi Arabia comes first which is the birth place of Mohammed, followed by Medina, where the Tomb of Mohammed is located.

The Church of the Holy Sepulcher is the holiest site for devout Christians. Inside the church is the Tomb of Christ which has room for four to five people at one time inside its enclosure. Devout Christians back out of the enclosure when leaving so that their back does not face the holy structure.

In developing the mural, pupils experience a plethora of salient literature on Jerusalem and its impotence to Three faiths. There is much interchange of ideas, orally, when pupils work on the mural. Len Vygotsky (1933 and 1978) stressed that learning is a social situation whereby ideas bounce off the minds of children when discussions occur.

Third, meaning is poignant when ideas are transmitted orally. Pupils need to understand what is taught. If content is not understood, pupils will turn off or listen with a lack of active involvement. Teachers need to be certain that pupils understand what is being taught. Having learners summarize in their own words facts, concepts, and generalizations, which were taught, will assist in evaluating if meaning was present. The summaries need to be comprehensive and communicated with clarity. Slovenly behaviour hinders effective transmission of messages from sender to the receiver (Ediger, 2013).

Fourth, resilience is a major factor in learning. Too frequently, pupils give up on completing an activity due to frustrations. Feelings of failure stand in the way of achievement. Thus, pupils should be taught to persevere in spite of obstacles. In school and in society, individuals face obstacles. These stumbling blocks cause hesitations and delays in sequential learnings. Learners need to face difficulties as challenges to persevere. The teacher may relate in his/her own lifetime when difficulties arose which needed to be overcome. Thus in speaking in front of a group, the presenter may feel very inept and incompetent. It is a belief or attitude which needs to be overcome. Here, the writer is relating experiences about the self when enrolled in a public speaking course as a freshmen enrolled in a teacher education sequence. He was not certain if he wanted to attend that first class session whereby each person introduced the self. Being very nervous, he attended and was the first class member, among seventeen to introduce himself. It went along alright, but it was a struggle. As the public speaking course continued, the class became more enjoyable, but there is still a fear of failure in public speaking. Doing what is good and feared at the same time is a situation in life faced by many. More confidence and feelings of success were gained when serving in teaching and doing relief work among Palestinian Arab refugees in Jordan, 1952-1954 with the Mennonite Central Committee, and upon return giving many slide presentations to religious and civic groups, as well as in schools. Feelings of success and a broad array of experiences assists in feeling resilient in spite of failures along the way. Resilience emphasizes bouncing back after experiencing failure, minor or major, is very poignant. In oral communication experiences, the teacher must supervise an environment which encourages resiliency. Ridiculing, putdowns, and rudeness must be eliminated so that each pupil feels free to participate in speaking and oral communication experiences.

Fifth, pupils self efficacy in achievement is of utmost importance. Here, pupils are supported by the teacher and peers in building self confidence. There are pupils who do not participate for fear of being minimized. Worthy praise, judiciously given, builds self confidence within an individual. Self confidence is needed to pursue challenges in life, be it in diverse activities and experiences. To reiterate each person will face mishaps and minor/major problems in life, and confidence is necessary to overcome obstacles in daily living. Individuals must learn to trust the self in decision making. High expectations with reasonable, achievable goals should be the lot for each person. To settle for mediocrity in life's endeavours robs the individual and society of innovations and improvements necessary for successful living (Ediger and Rao, 2014).

Sixth, technology needs to be adopted which will assist more optimal learner progress. Technological utilization needs to assist in attaining objectives of instruction. The inherent learning opportunities guide in attaining these worthy ends. Assessment emphasizes how effective the technological adaptations worked in the curriculum. Oral communication must be/is inherent in each learning activity.

REFERENCES

Ediger, Marlow (2013), "Philosophies of Reading Instruction," Reading Improvement, 50 (3), 132-134.

Ediger, Marlow, and D. Bhaskara Rao (2014), The Curriculum of School Subjects. New Delhi, India: Discovery Publishing House.

Vygotsky, Len (1933 and 1978), Mind in Society: The Development of Higher Psychological Processes. Cambridge, Massachusetts: Harvard University Press.

CHAPTER 12
Oral Communication, Teacher and Pupil

Oral communication is a skill that integrates well within all academic disciplines and is poignant in school and in society. Clarity is necessary in order to send messages in an oral manner from the sender to the receiver of the contents. Each person has stated ideas which were not comprehended effectively. Individuals need to improve in communicating well with others so that better listening might come about. The speaker has an obligation to communicate meaningfully so that the listener might well understand that which was said orally. It is necessary to take part in various assignments, tasks, and opportunities during the pubic school years so that the person on the job or in entering college has met standards of proficiency in oral communication. Thus beginning in the pre-school years and moving toward secondary school graduation, the person has mastered needed concepts, skills, and attitudes toward making subject matter known to participants.

Oral Communication in the Curriculum

In each class pursued in the public schools, oral communication activities need to abound. Authentic activities should receive precedence in that these are lifelike and relevant. Problem solving is a key component then of the oral communications curriculum; brain storming is a major inherent learning activity. The committee involved is tackling a problem related to an ongoing unit of study; the members should consist of four classmates who are able to work together. In skeletal form, the committee with teacher assistance needs to orally:

- identify and clarify the problem so it is solvable.

- discuss poignant reference sources in working toward a solution.
- collectively develop an hypothesis, directly related to the problem.
- test the hypothesis in as realistic situation as possible.
- revise and modify the hypothesis if necessary (Ediger and Rao, 2014).

The classroom teacher is a guide in assisting pupils to stay on task, move forward sequentially, and present ideas clearly. All members should participate, but no one dominate committee endeavours. Leadership needs to emerge within the committee with a chosen recorder. A chairperson might be selected, if desired. Committee members need to sequence their own work with teacher guidance. They should report periodically to other committees in providing a progress summary.

Large group as well as collaborative endeavours, also, need to stress the saliency of appropriate standards in oral communication. Active involvement by all needs to be emphasized to notice wholehearted interests in the activity. Domination by a few must be interspersed and made room for all respondents in the class. When supervising university student teachers in the public schools, the writer experienced that too many pupils are left out of a discussion. For each pupil to achieve well, learners individually must have opportunities to participate. The teacher needs to encourage shy and non-participants to engage in the discussions. If the latter two do not take part, the chances are they will feel left out of large group discussions. They might not even read the printed materials which provide necessary background information. Learning is sequential in all endeavours, oral communication included.

Confidence building is salient and pupils develop feelings of confidence by being successful in ongoing experiences. Praise provided judiciously may encourage fuller participation. Praise such as, "I like your answer," invites further participation.

Nothing curtails active involvement more than ridiculing of answers/responses; this includes rude behaviour, sarcasm, and put downs, among other negative responses by the teacher or pupils.

Providing a variety of oral experiences is needed for pupils to achieve proficiency in this area, which includes reports to the class. A report on a topic related to the ongoing unit may well provide the stimulus. The report needs to be meaningful to listeners, otherwise turning off will occur. The pace of the presentation must harmonize with listener attention span. An orderly arrangement of contents needs to be in evidence. Jumping around from one idea to another unrelated idea hinders listener attention and might well make for confusion in their minds. Thus, the oral report needs to be:

- interesting to capture listener attention.
- understandable to make for listener comprehension.
- possessive of voice inflection with proper stress and pitch of words.
- grammatically correct in terms of word and sentence usage.

Proper eye contact with listeners is salient. Each of these goals listed above will be incremental in achievement and progress by the presenter of the report. Continuous headways must then be made.

Learning to give directions is poignant. In society, people are asked to give accurate directions to a specific place. In school, it is vital to provide clear and distinct directions for playing a game, for getting served in the school cafeteria, for classroom conduct and behaviour, and in doing daily activities in the curriculum, among other tasks. The teacher then needs to provide pupil's with experiences involved in the giving of directions. A question arises, "Are children able to follow directions for playing a creative game developed by a committee or by an individual learner?" Each game developed must be assessed using appropriate criteria, a major criterion being ***clarity*** in providing directions for others to follow.

There are a multitude of additional suggestions involving learning experiences pertaining to oral communication which include the following:

- creative and formal dramatizations.
- vocabulary study from ongoing lessons and units of study. These relevant words might then be recorded with accompanying definitions and within contextual sentences.
- public speaking on selected topics at parent/teacher association meetings.
- writing and reciting poetry and verse.
- participating in debates.
- reading aloud to classmates (Ediger, 2013).

Conclusion

Pupils need to experience a wide variety of oral communication activities which are useful in school and in society. Objectives of instruction in oral communication need to be clear and sequential. Learning activities must be aligned with the objectives, and a high quality assessment program must be in evidence to ascertain learner progress.

REFERENCES

Ediger, Marlow, and D. Bhaskara Rao (2014), School Subjects, Issues and Concerns. New Delhi, India: Discovery Publishing House.

Ediger, Marlow (2013), "The Teacher and Students in the Social Studies," College Student Journal, 47 (4), 649 652.

CHAPTER 13

Listening Across Curriculum

Listening as a skills objective must be emphasize throughout the curriculum of school subjects. There are a variety of learning opportunities which stress the art and skills of listening. In conversation, it might be embarrassing if the sender of the message needs to repeat content due to faulty listening habits. Or, the responder in response says things which are unrelated to what the speaker has said. Courtesy is involved in being a good listener. Objectives pertaining to high quality listening skills need to permeate each academic discipline taught.

Listening and Oral Communication are Complimentary

There are a plethora of occasions in which individuals engage in listening to others; this is true in school and in society. Listening skills transfer well to life in society. At the work place, individuals must be good listeners to receive salient messages as well as communicate effectively. Thus, too frequently, errors are made in oral transactions due to faulty listening.

Teachers need to plan carefully to include listening objectives in teaching and learning situations across the curriculum.

Goal number one should stress a purpose within the ongoing learning opportunity. Purposes deal with a reason or reasons, clearly articulated by the teacher, as to why a solution to multi-step problems in mathematics is salient. The teacher might state the importance of not losing out on any one sequential step since ensuing knowledge here is based upon what is presently known. This needs to be clearly demonstrated by the teacher. A purpose may also be made on selected errors made in the previously lesson completed by learners with the teacher showing specifically where the error(s) were made. Thus, the pupil needs to be aware of ongoing reasons for participating in a learning opportunity. Careful, goal centered listening is involved in thee experiences.

Goal number two emphasizes the importance of the interest factor in learning. The kind of activity chosen as well as the method of instruction will hinder or assist in developing good listening habits. Interest in the learning opportunity promotes effort in achieving. The inherent discussions provide situations involving improved listening. Dull, uninspiring activities hinder listening progress. Motivation, as well as effort accrue with high quality learning opportunities (Ediger, 2007).

Goal number three stresses the importance of challenge in pupils becoming better listeners. High expectations, but attainable, should be the order of the day. The teacher must take notice if pupil achievement is increasing in listening skills. Much time is wasted if assignments, for example, need to be repeated continuously due to improper listening. Directions should be given clearly and concisely; these may be printed on the chalkboard so that pupils who did not get the directions orally, might receive them in print. This should aid in listening improvement in that the directions are not repetitiously repeated. Then too, pupils might be asked to state the directions orally after they have been provided by the teacher, as an approach to assess listening comprehension.

Goal number four emphasizes pupils having numerous opportunities to listen and to improve therein. Whole class discussions assist pupils in practicing listening skills as well as to interact with classmates. There are general rules which need to be followed such as, as many need to participate as possible. Marginalizing a few from participation is not acceptable.

In small group or committee endeavours, pupils may engage in problem solving whereby careful listening is required. Ideas bounce off the minds of participants in learning as they participate (Vygotsky, 1933-1978). Problem solving involves deliberation and thought in developing an hypothesis directly related to an identified relevant problem area. The hypothesis needs evaluation in terms of adequate data/information gathered, resulting in accepting or refuting the hypothesis. The hypothesis might also be modified or a new one developed. To engage in problem solving experiences requires careful listening to contributions made. The small group approach also needs evaluation of performance in terms of carefully Grafted criteria. Listening carefully to comments made is a major component of the assessment. Once pupils realize weaknesses in listening, they will tend to improve achievement. Careful listening is related to clarity of ideas presented in the ongoing activity.

Goal number five stresses the saliency of listening carefully in general matters pertaining to school improvement. Thus within parent/teacher conferences, be they formal or very informal, it is poignant to listen carefully to what the parent is communicating. The communication provides valuable content, many times, for teaching and learning situations. A hobby, for instance, possessed by the child provides information to build upon in his/her curriculum.

It is salient to provide information to important decision makers on school policy. Hot topic items here include teacher evaluation methods and means, compensation for services performed, supplies necessary for quality teaching, as well as the need for counseling and guidance services in school. Then too, there are needs of the teacher such as the following which need to be communicated to policy makers:

- tenure maintenance.
- necessity of educational technology to achieve objectives of instruction.
- length of school day as in adding 30 minutes to each day of school.
- inservice education related proposals.
- need for summer school (Ediger and Rao, 2014).

When discussing each of the above asterisked items, it is quite obvious that communicated content may be misunderstood due to poor listening habits. Clarification of presented needs is to be emphasized, when necessary. Condescending remarks, rude statements, and self righteous attitudes must be omitted. Good listening is a must!

REFERENCES

Ediger, Marlow (2007), "Meaning in Reading Instruction," Reading Improvement, 44 (4), 217-220.

Ediger, Marlow, and D. Bhaskara Rao (2014), The Curriculum of School Subjects: Issues and Concerns. New Delhi, India: Discovery Publishing House.

Vygotsky, Len (1933, 1978), The Development of Higher Psychological Processes. Cambridge, Massachusetts: Harvard University Press.

CHAPTER 14

Listening in Language Arts

Listening is a very salient facet of learning. We learn much from others through listening. In school and in society, individuals interact verbally with others; thus pupils need much experience in developing meticulous listening skills in the language arts.

Listening has often been minimized and needs adequate emphasis as an objective of instruction, which cuts across all academic and curriculum areas. Thus, all teachers must stress the importance of listening skills in the school setting. Too many times, knowledge and skills are repeated in school due to inadequacy in listening skills (Ediger, 2011).

Emphasizing Listening in Teaching and Learning Situations

How might listening be stressed in ensuing learning experiences? Inservice education must be in evidence which targets listening within subject matter taught. Strong leadership is needed to develop a series of meetings devoted to inservice education to promote listening. From these meetings, definite techniques and methods of instruction must cater to trying out ideas presented within inservice programs. Meaning must be attached to each idea so that it is usable in classroom settings. Feedback to the inservice group might tend to be perceived as having possibilities with queries raised and modifications made. Thus, listening as integrated in to the curriculum has value to many teachers and support personnel.

Workshops which emphasize the interest factor in teaching which holds and maintains pupil attention is paramount. In supervising university student teachers in the public schools, the writer noticed, what he deemed to be carefully planned interesting activities, which seemingly did not capture the attention of selected pupils. The teacher must try to obtain learner interests at all times. Learning activities may need changing, as the need arises, to meet the criterion of interest.

Second, pupils need to perceive relevancy in subject matter being listened to. There is much content expressed in school and in society which provide opportunities for listening; however, learners must perceive relevancy and involving practicality. This presents difficulties to implement; however, pupils desire to learn what will be of assistance in life's endeavours. Problems exist and these need identification. They should be problems which pupils see as being important. In finding solutions, pupils need to think of tentative hypotheses; these may be listed for all to see and might well become a brain storming experience. Careful listening is inherent in attaining unexpressed hypothesis at this point. Needed research from a variety of sources, including the internet, might provide a selected solution. Debate and indepth discussions are necessary. Pupils need to listen carefully when testing the hypotheses from the evaluated information acquired. This is necessary in order to rationally and objectively modify, accept, or refute the hypothesis.

Third, there is not a more salient reason for not listening than not understanding the facts, concepts, and generalizations being expressed. Teachers and peers need to make certain that subject matter expressed possesses clarity and understanding. That is one salient method of interaction in large, small, and individual endeavours in discussion with others. It is a waste of time if meaning cannot be attached to ongoing lessons and units of study. Pacing of ideas expressed need to be adequate and harmonize with what a pupil can comprehend. Appropriate stress, pitch, and pauses need attention to encourage quality listening. Frequently, too much rapidity in speaking as well as a shrill monotone voice are in evidence which hinders quality listening. There is much the teacher can do to assist pupils to improve listening skills.

Fourth, pupils need considerable practice in developing the skills and art of good listening habits. Individual learners need to be asked to state a summary of what was discussed in the lesson just completed. Here, Pupils realize they will be held accountable for being quality listeners. The summary asked for might be brief, but must contain salient subject matter. The teacher needs to model the objective of listening to develop a summary of expressed ideas.

Respect for others is poignant in these situations. Being ridiculed and minimized for what was said hinders being a good listener and will prevent presenting good summary statements. The writer is a firm believer in having good human relations in the school setting which is of utmost importance in any successes generated by the learner and felt by the teacher. Rudeness, put downs, and name calling need eliminating. Children should not emulate what transpires in society such as:

- name calling. In news reports, an individual is called a communist, a Hitlerite, among others.
- freedom of speech is exaggerated when saying a minor incident of the opposite political party is "like a train wreck" or worse than the "Holocaust."
- sarcasm directed toward a person of the opposite persuasion.
- intimidation so that freedom of speech is hindered. Bullying and harassment are forms of intimidation (Ediger, 2013).

Listening carefully to appraise an oral presentation is an important factor and goal to emphasize. Activities such as the following may be stressed here:

- the teacher presenting subject matter aloud with selected errors made. Pupils need to listen meticulously to detect each error.
- pupils placing their heads on his/her desk, enfolded by the arms, so that they cannot see what is being presented directly in back of them. The teacher makes certain

sounds for pupils to identify such as crushing a sheet of waste paper, pouring water from one cup to another, and tapping the foot.

- whispering a phrase for pupil identification.

Critical listening is a major goal to emphasize. Pupils with teacher guidance need to be able to listen carefully to separate facts from opinions, fantasy from reality, as well as accurate from inaccurate content and ideas. Certainly, detecting bias is highly poignant as a goal. In a democracy, freedom to express oneself is advocated. This can certainly cross the line and go to the extreme. Politicians verbally state extremist points of view in some cases. For example, one state legislator in Kansas advocated that parents should determine what is taught and how it is to be taught. Even in this one statement, the following questions might be raised:

- Do parents have that much knowledge to know what is right in terms of knowledge needed by children and also appropriate methods of instruction? There would be wide disagreement here.
- Are parents that much of a role model in doing the advocating? After all, much crime is committed and misdeeds are committed by adults in society.

Too frequently, opposing sides desire to silence the opposition. Wheres in a democracy, open discussions without fear is an ideal.

REFERENCES

Ediger, Marlow (2011), "Collaboration Versus Individual Endeavours in the Curriculum" Education, 132 (1), 217-220.

Ediger, Marlow (2013), "The Teacher and Students in the Social Studies," College Student Journal, 47 (4), 649-652.

CHAPTER 15 Writing in Language Arts

There are selected pointers for teachers to follow in emphasizing writing activities in the language arts. These are guidelines in assisting pupils to achieve more optimally in written work.

First, pupils need to perceive relevance in the ongoing experience. Too frequently, writing in the language arts is assigned and when completed, teachers read and evaluate the completed work. There must be more of purpose inherent in that learners communicate salient content to others with an ensuing response to the written product. To make contact in the written product, the sender has worthwhile ideas to communicate. Thus, the teacher must assist pupils to sense reasons for communication, such as in the following:

- inviting parents to attend a local Parent/Teachers Association meeting. The class as a whole or a committee might brainstorm what should go into the communique. To communicate clearly the results of the brainstorming might well include the what (PTA meeting), the where (place of meeting, when (exact time), why (purpose of the meeting), and who is invited.
- e-mailing parents in terms of ongoing lesson/unit content being studied.
- writing a friendly letter or a business letter to be mailed.
- doing a Letter to the Editor pertaining to a needed improvement in the community.
- writing poem directly related to what is being studied in mathematics, science, social studies. The poem might be unrhymed as in free verse or contain rhyme as in a limerick or quatrain, and should be shared with classmates.
- summarizing what has been learned in a unit of study.

Second, interest needs to be poignant in written work. If pupils are to critically appraise an essay, the teacher needs to develop interest in this activity. Sharing a personal appraisal with learners indicates that "it is good only for thee, but also for me." Being enthusiastic, in writing on the teacher's part, is generally reflected within pupils. Enthusiastic learners provide for effort and resilience in writing. Proper voice inflection utilized in teaching in terms of stress and pitch as well as voice enunciation aids in making a lesson interesting. In supervising university student teachers in the public schools, the writer has noticed student and cooperating teachers being able to motivate pupils in writing with high quality methodology used in the instructional arena so that learners volunteer on their own to do more writing. This was done with intrinsic rewards being used. Thus, a questioning procedure which lead to increased pupil writing for a variety of reasons was used. In contrast heavy use of externally rewarding pupils in one school with thirteen pupils in the classroom was being emphasized. Thus in using a language arts workbook, for each correct response to a numbered item, the cooperating or university student teacher placed a Santa Claus inked rubber stamp. This was possible due to the two teachers being available for thirteen pupils! Pupils did desire to have the rubber stamped Santa Claus appear a plethora of times on a workbook page. The feelings of reward may fade if used extensively.

Third meaningful activities need to be prevalent in written work. To reiterate, the handing in of completed work for the teacher, alone, to see and appraise is not adequate. With meaningful experiences, the teacher, parents, and pupils communicate with each other in numerous ways. The communique needs to possess meaning in that it conveys, sends, and responds, with salient information such as invitation to a birthday party, open house invitation, to a parent/teacher organization meeting. A friendly letter message is always welcome.

With more formal writing activities, the teacher needs to stimulate pupil meaning in writing summaries, reports, outlines, and reviews. The content must make sense to the sender as well as receiver of the written communication.

CHAPTER 16

Salient Pointers in Teaching Reading

Trends in reading instruction may come and go, but there are poignant factors in the teaching of reading which are rather consistent to emphasize. Reading teachers need to stress that which remains salient and yet leave room for studying what might become important. Being a continuous student of studying trends in reading instruction through workshops, attendance at International Reading Association state and national conventions, taking course work at accredited universities, and doing much reading from reputable journals, among others, help teachers to develop feelings of self efficacy.

Pointers in Teaching and Learning

Which factors then make for a high quality program of reading instruction? First, pupils need to become self sufficient in word recognition. Context clues might well be utilized in determining words which appear to be unknown. Within the context of reading a given selection, the pupil needs to substitute a meaningful word for the unknown; many times this will take care of recognizing specific words. If it does not, then viewing the first letter, generally being a consonant, will provide further assistance. Additional phonic learnings may be stressed as necessary. Beginning reading instruction might well stress the utilization of E-books whereby the content is read aloud with pupils following along in the printed script. Learning to read is then emphasized through the sight method and interspersed phonics. If E-books are not available, then a "big" book with large print may be used in which the teacher reads aloud a few pages, pointing to involved words. A small group of six or seven are taught at one time whereby all can see each word clearly as it is being read. Pupils in sequence read aloud together without the teacher, the same contents, noticing each word carefully; fluency in reading, however, must be emphasized. Rereading may be done as often as needed to assist pupils to develop skills in reading.

Second, pupils need to comprehend subject matter read, satisfactorily. Close reading is stressed. When questions arise, the answers sought initially should come from the text for verification purposes. This might well involve reading the same contents again for accuracy in comprehension. In sequence, other texts might be used to make for comparisons. Also, learners achieve skills in word recognition and meaning when rereading the same contents. To reiterate, comparisons may follow with information gleaned from related reference sources.

Third, pupils need background information prior to reading ensuing subject matter. The accompanying visual aids within the text and brief discussions pertaining thereto should conjure interest within the learner in wanting to read. With this information, pupils understand more thoroughly the related abstract content. It might become relatively easier to identify unknown words on a page by viewing the illustration(s) with the utilization of picture clues. This is especially true for primary grade pupils whereby illustrations are more in evidence in reading materials. The goal is to assist learners to become good reader who comprehend well, in addition to learning from pictures (Ediger, 2013).

Fourth, problem solving must receive emphasis to encourage indepth learning. Ideally, the problem should come from pupils in ongoing lessons and units of study. The problem needs to be adequately delimited so it is solvable. Brain storming techniques might be used to develop an hypothesis. These should be recorded on the white board so that all involved may see each hypothesis clearly. Adequate interest in achievement is then in evidence. Hypotheses need testing by using relevant reference sources. The hypothesis may be revised, if need be; new problems also might come into being. Problem solving activities take time for adequate research, appraisal of possible solutions, and seeking what is relevant. The teacher helps, guides, and encourages pupils to be on their own in these types of experiences.

Fifth, critical thinking must be stressed. Thus, pupils separate facts from opinions, accurate from inaccurate ideas, as well as fantasy from reality. Creative thinking also has its poignancy in that pupils need to come up with unique, novel ideas. Creative thinking cuts across all curriculum areas and should be a major goal of instruction. Additional kinds of thinking involve inferential thought.

Sixth, pupils need to read semi-concrete materials which are generally embedded within abstract words. These include pictures and illustrations, referred to previously; charts such as vocabulary, classification, and process; graphs including bar, line, and circle; time lines; diagrams; and tables of information.

Seventh, rational balance must be in evidence between information and narrative reading materials. The focus should not be upon emphasizing one to the exclusion of the other. An educated person has received guidelines for living from both. Education is a lifelong process whereby forgetting and hazy thinking might well occur unless the individual is a continuous student of learning (Ediger and Rao, 2014).

REFERENCES

Ediger, Marlow (2013), Philosophies of Reading Instruction, Reading Improvement, 50 (3), 132-135.

Ediger, Marlow, and D. Bhaskara Rao (2014), School Subjects, Issues and Concerns. New Delhi, India: Discovery Publishing House.

CHAPTER 17

Teaching of Reading and Its New Emphasis

Teachers and supervisors of reading instruction need to stay abreast of trends and concerns when assisting pupils to achieve more optimally. Reading which meets high expectations is needed in school and in society. Thus, professionals involved in teaching reading in different academic and curriculum areas need to utilize the best methods of instruction possible. Wholehearted involvement by each pupil is necessary for goal attainment as well as for personal enrichment in reading. What makes for a quality reading program in the school setting?

Providing for Individual Differences

Pupils differ from each other in a plethora of ways such as in reading achievement, abilities, and background information. What learners bring to the reading curriculum is as salient as is that which is brought to them. Thus, it is cognizant for teachers and supervisors to study each pupil carefully in order to ascertain sequential experiences. Providing experiences which might well take care of deficiencies or encourage passions in ongoing lessons and units of study are important. Sequence is relevant when providing necessary information and skills directly related to an ensuing lesson. If information presented here is completely foreign or vague, it is unlikely that pupils will benefit much from the new subject matter to be acquired. Or, if poorly presented, pupils may be limited in applying ideas to the ensuing. Clarity is a salient concept to emphasize in the instructional arena.

Second, pupils need to learn to read information carefully. Too frequently, survey approaches have been utilized, making for shallow understandings of facts, concepts, and generalizations. *Close* reading is then necessary whereby the author's meaning becomes poignant. Questions which arise during the reading from the text need indepth or close reading. Rereading might well provide necessary subject matter for verification of answers. Additional reference sources may then be brought in as feasible to secure information to identified questions. Thinking is a major goal in reading instruction; thus, learners must be challenged as well as encouraged to develop thinking skills. Higher levels of cognition are then involved which resonate throughout instruction. Critical thinking and problem solving are major avenues of stressing thinking in its diverse dimensions. The teacher needs to model aloud critical thinking skills such as analyzing into component parts and this includes separation of information in terms of being factual versus opinion, accurate versus inaccurate content, and the relevant from the irrelevant. Verbal modeling of problem solving includes problem identification and clarification, developing an hypothesis, as well as testing and evaluating the hypothesis (Ediger, 2014).

Third, word recognition needs adequate teaching and learning activities. Fluency is an ultimate objective in reading; however, to realize this goal, pupils need to use context clues and phonic skills. Context clues assist pupils in making sense in attempting to identify a word for the unknown. Each attempted word must make sense in relationship to the rest of the wording in the sentence or paragraph. Further assistance is provided when sound symbol relationships or phonics is put into operation in order to recognize an unknown word. There is consistency between selected letters and their corresponding sounds, such as the following, for example, b, d, f, l, m, whereas letter combinations such as "ph" as in phone, ch as in chair, need to be learned as sight sounds. The teacher must choose an appropriate methodology to teach words with sounds which are phonetically consistent between sound and symbol and those which are non-phonetic.

Fourth, comprehension is the ultimate goal of reading instruction. Phonics and syllabication are means to an end and that being-comprehension. To reiterate, comprehension involves higher levels of cognition involving critical thinking and problem solving as well as creative thought, among others. To whet pupil appetites in literary content, the teacher needs to read aloud in an enthusiastic and meaningful manner, information as well as narrative accounts to learners during story hour. Pupils of all ability levels may benefit from listening to the content. This encourages pupils to read on their own during allotted time in class as well as in the home setting. Reading for sheer enjoyment aids pupils in achieving major skills and attitudes toward literature.

Fifth, a variety of procedures should be utilized to asses achievement in reading. Teacher observation might well be an excellent approach if updated criteria are used. This might provide continuous information on word recognition achievement, components in comprehension, fluency in reading, and general attitudes toward reading narrative and information sources. Standardized tests, valid and reliable, provide feedback on general reading progress. Printouts of each pupil's test results assist in pinpointing specific types of difficulties that a pupil might experience. These may be used as ***summative*** since end of the year results will be given. ***Formative*** tests, as compared to summative testing, are administered prior to summative tests and provide feedback to the teacher in terms of what needs to be emphasized within the unit of study which is still ongoing. These are valuable results since corrections may still be made in ensuing activities within an instructional sequence (Ediger, 2013).

Conclusion

A high quality reading program needs to be in the offing for all pupils. Teachers and supervisors need to follow recommended procedures of instruction. Inservice education is necessary to stay abreast of recommended teaching and learning methodology.

REFERENCES

Ediger, Marlow (2014), "Science and Reading Within Indepth Problem Solving," Edutracks,13 (5), 3-4.

Ediger, Marlow (2013), "Philosophies of Reading Instruction," Reading Improvement, 50 (3), 132-134.

CHAPTER 18 Social Studies Curriculum and the C3 Framework

As society changes, so must the social studies embrace innovations and modifications. The pupil needs to accept societal changes with the view that he/she must stress good citizenship in a changing world. The C3 Framework emphasizes readiness for career, college, and civics. As pupils move forward throughout the grades, they will study different social studies units emphasizing salient knowledge and skills. Useful understandings are necessary to achieve a well rounded person, capable of making quality decisions. Good attitudes will be a by product in goal attainment. Flexible thinking within alternatives is necessary to function well in the societal realm (Ediger and Rao, 2012).

C3 Framework and the Social Studies

Inquiry methods are at the heart of the framework and need indepth approaches in teaching and learning situations. Pupils need to perceive the interaction of ideas among the involved academic disciplines in the social studies. A questioning approach stimulates learner curiosity and interest in ongoing lessons and units of study. Here, pupils have opportunities to achieve vital facts, concepts, and generalizations with learners having chances to make application of subject matter being acquired. Relevant content achieved, then, has utilitarian values, not for the sake of its learning, but for use in the social studies and in society. The new social studies stresses challenging experiences for pupils to up progress in learning since it was minimized under the No Child Left Behind (NCLB) law of 2002 which basically emphasized the language arts and mathematics, with science added on later (Ediger, 2011).

The C3 Framework might well be an integral part of the Common Core State Standards (CCSS) which has emphasized close reading as a key component. In the area of history, for example, pupils do a considerable amount of reading, including primary and secondary sources, whereby close reading is to be stressed. Thus, careful reading of text materials must be in the offing such as in the following:

- pupils verifying from the text, answers to questions raised pertaining to content read.
- rereading subject matter to make for quality comprehension and understanding. Indepth learning is emphasized.
- attaching meaning to graphs, charts, and tables, embedded in ensuing subject matter.
- assuming the role of an historian in ongoing learning opportunities.
- reading for main ideas, subordinate content, and details in developing structure in reading abstract subject matter from the different social science disciplines. A variety of learning activities should be utilized in teaching to provide for individual differences; These may include dramatic experiences (formal and informal) which breathes life into content being studied, use of time lines and simulations, reading biographies and autobiographies, internet sources in securing needed information, as well as oral histories of local people.

An interdisciplinary social science curriculum needs to be emphasized when this assists pupils to achieve meaningfully in ongoing its of study. Thus, when studying historical units of study, the pupil needs to make connections with the following academic disciplines:

- geography to notice where events took place. Here, pupils study people interaction with the planet earth, identify homogeneous regions such as the Mediterranean world, how people modify the earth, as well as physical characteristics and place location.

- political science in carefully noting which laws, rules and regulations were in vogue. Rules need development for the classroom in emphasizing democracy as a way of life. Cooperative and collaborative behaviour stresses the saliency of individuals working together harmoniously.
- economics in studying prevailing systems of producing goods and services at the time of unit study. The Hutterite Mennonites, living in Montana, California, South and North Dakota, among other states and Canada offer opportunities to study a communal economic system in the Unites States. In each Hutterite commune of thirty families, all property is owned in common. Each person therein works for the good of the commune and not for individual gains. A Hutterite minister heads each commune, followed by a business manager who deals with the outside world in securing the best buys for farm machinery and equipment. He also is in charge of selling agricultural produts from farming. In addition, the work supervisor assigns members to different tasks in the rural commune. Four families live per apartment on the commune with no individual kitchen facilities. A communal kitchen is used to feed all commune members with mothers and small children seated at one extended table, whereas fathers eat at a separate table with older children seated separately.

Each person is to contribute to his/her utmost, not for personal gains. Children are taught on the commune.

- sociology/anthropology in learning about how cultural factors influenced human behaviour. Parker (2001), provides the following structural ideas which may permeate throughout the social studies curriculum:
  1. Every society has formed its own system of beliefs, knowledge, values, and traditions which can be called its culture.

2. Culture is socially learned and serves a potential guide for human behaviour in any society.
3. Although people everywhere are confronted with similar psychological and physiological needs, the ways in which they meet these needs differ according to their culture.
4. The art, music, architecture, food, clothing, sports, and customs of a people help to produce a national identity.

A study of Old Order Amish culture should assist pupils to realize the poignancy of values and how they are handed down from generation to generation with their customs of dress and appearance. Amish women, for example, wear plain coloured dresses extending down to the ankles, with a high neckline and long sleeves. A prayer cap is worn by Amish women continuously. Horse drain implements are generally used by Amish farmers to pull grain drills for seeding crops, for plowing the fields after the grain has been harvested, for harrowing to smooth the farm land after plowing, and for pulling a grain binder to make bundles of the grain ripe crops. Tradition is stressed, not modernism, and is shown in farming methods as well as in means of transportation. Thus in transportation carriages pulled by horses are utilized instead of automobiles. Large families of six to eight children are wanted as an ideal. Social needs are met through visiting within the Old Order Amish community as well as in church attendance in homes and barns, followed by fellowship meals.

Civics (political science) and its implications must be emphasized throughout the time a unit is taught. Thus, learners study and implement what a good citizen does in school and in society. Simulated voting in the classroom must be stressed, with thorough developmental knowledge being inherent in making decisions among candidates. Understanding the laws, rules, and regulations in the nation, state, and local levels are salient and need to be abided by. Respect and acceptance of others as well as feelings of empathy need emphasis in ongoing lessons and units of study. Appreciation of benefits in the societal realm and giving back to the community makes for a well rounded individual.

Conclusion

There are a plethora of ingredients which go into a quality C3 Framework Social Studies program of instruction. These are intermingled in making the best decisions possible in choosing objectives for pupil achievement, learning opportunities to achieve these ends, as well as appraisal procedures to ascertain if the chosen objectives have been realized.

REFERENCES

Ediger, Marlow (2012), Essays in Teaching Social Studies, New Delhi, India: Discovery Publishing House.

Ediger, Marlow (2011), "Meaning in the Social Studies," College Student Journal, 45 (2), 233-237.

Parker, Walter C. (2001), Social Studies in Elementary Education. Columbus, Ohio: Merrill, Prentice, 132.

CHAPTER 19

Teaching Social Studies, An Indepth Approach

Social studies has been neglected with it not be emphasized in NCLB testing in that what is tested is what will be taught. Being tested with NCLB tests also has its harmful effects due to factual items lending themselves to test taking. Multiple choice test items in NCLB make for rote learning and memorization in reports from different school systems whereby teachers may spend weeks drilling pupils on subject matter knowledge and the art of test taking. Better it is to emphasize higher levels of cognition in teaching and learning situations. Drilling pupils for taking a test does not make for enduring and thoughtful learning, but stresses regurgitation of subject matter which is of little possible use. Thus, unconnected bits of information are to accrue when pupils respond to multiple choice test items. Instead, social studies instruction must emphasize joy and excitement in learning. Pupils making discoveries and identifying problems and questions makes for a relevant social studies curriculum.Then too, learners need to make choices and decisions. Life consists of choosing from among alternatives (Ediger and Rao, 2012).

Developing the Social Studies Curriculum

Curriculum design in the social studies needs to be ongoing and continuous. Teachers and supervisors need to be on the lookout for ways of improvement in objectives, learning opportunities, and appraisal procedures. To live in a technological age requires that individuals be knowledgeable, interested, and perceive purpose in improving society. The author was born in 1927 when his family drove a Model A Ford with a starter when some used a hand crank to start the car. There were no heaters in these cars and the windshield wiper had to be operated by hand. They drove about 35 miles per hour and started to vibrate when driven a little bit faster. In 1937, my parents bought a 1937 Plymouth and what a joy it was to have a heater in the car. The windshield wiper was electrically operated and kept the windshield free from rain and defrosted the windows for better vision in winter. The maximum speed driven was, approximately, 45-50 miles per hour. The car battery "ran down" very quickly when starting the car on a cold day. Our grange, attached to the barn, had a little hill, making it possible to push it downhill to start the car with a mechanical gear shift.

Compare the above with new car models which:

- can readily go 85 miles per hour easily, readily defying speed limits.
- have air conditioning and excellent heaters as standard equipment; the engine starts even when temperature readings fall to/below 20 degrees Fahrenheit.
- ride very smoothly at almost any speed and all have good radios. Our 1937 Plymouth had no radio and very few cars did at that time.
- power steering, automatic drive, and power brakes, among other features.

So much for the above comparisons in automobiles. This says to us that the curriculum also must change in time. I Pads are four to five years since their inception with many schools having adopted them for many classes. My high school of graduation, Inman, Kansas (city of eleven hundred people) purchased I Pads for all students for the 2011-2012 school year, with many technological advances already in place.

With much knowledge available, pupils need guidance to focus on major ideas, not trivia nor irrelevant facts. This attempts to answer the question in broad outline, "What should be taught?" Key ideas provide structure in learning as well as a framework for pupils studying each structure, carefully defined and developed, with intensified teaching. Supporting subject matter give strength to each structural idea.

A variety of kinds of learning opportunities must be provided. Each activity reinforces those inherent ideas, making for indepth teaching. Careful and meticulous sequencing provides opportunities for success in pupil achievement. Ensuing subject matter acquired, based upon what was taught previously, directly relates the new with the old in concepts and generalizations taught. Then too, learning by discovery makes for excitement as well as interest in achievement. Instead of lecture, pupil involvement invites learner questions and problem identification. This does involve brain storming in a plethora of cases. With inquiry methods of instruction, pupil collaboration is needed whereby they:

- stay on the topic unless additional worthwhile problems are selected and identified.
- respect and accept each other as human beings and not as objects.
- contribute, individually, to the ongoing discussion to make for indepth learning.
- summarize conclusions to use in new or novel situations.
- do something with learnings acquired such as writing creative verse and poetry, making a classroom booklet of main ideas obtained, keeping diary and/or log entries.
- do an art project, mural, frieze, among other visual arts, pertaining to indepth generalizations and concepts (Ediger, 2009).

Reading in the Social Studies

Pupils need to read primary sources. These are original in its entirety and written by a eye witness account. One of the writer's graduate students brought to class a diary with the actual dated accounts of a Civil War relative. The handwriting was clear on the aged yellow pages revealing the style used at that time. Some of the content, the diary writer wrote, was in an abbreviated form, but was generally decipherable. This was read aloud by the teacher as students followed along on the clearly legible screen. There was considerable excitement and interest in the diary contents. Several sessions were spent on its reading and discussion, along with other internet primary sources. Students learned how to integrate and relate primary sources with ongoing units of study.

Secondary sources are good to use, providing they are accurate and on the reading levels of involved learners. These secondary sources include carefully chosen basal textbooks, as well as information based library books. Different word recognition techniques need to be emphasized for those pupils needing assistance in identifying the unknown. These include context and picture clues, phonics, and syllabication. Content analysis is definitely salient in order to aid indepth comprehension. This includes:

- reading to secure vital facts.
- reading to obtain poignant concepts and generalization.
- reading for a sequence of ideas.
- reading to appraise subject matter.
- reading to compare/contrast sources of information.
- reading to analyze and synthesize subject matter.
- reading to perceive cause/effect relationships.

Subject matter secured must be discussed indepth involving critical and creative thought. Relevant subject matter and discussions provide a plethora of opportunities to utilize what has been learned. The total social studies curriculum must emphasize developing the good citizen and this needs to be stressed with poignant subject matter knowledge, model behaviour during classroom endeavors as well as in the school setting. Respect for others is always important!

Evaluation of Achievement

Diverse procedures need to be utilized in indepth unit instruction in the social studies. Teacher observation of pupil behavior in ongoing lessons and units of study in terms of definite standards of conduct. Assessing pupil products in the classroom/school setting, directly related to a social studies unit, should be emphasized. A carefully developed rubric may be developed and used here. Teacher written tests help the teacher in formative and summative evaluation ascertain what has been mastered and what needs additional teaching and learning. Pupil self evaluation, using a carefully devised score card, guides pupils in achieving more optimal progress. Additional appraisal procedures should include the following:

- standardized tests which measure social studies achievement in subject matter knowledge as well as in thinking skills and in attitudinal development.
- diagnostic tests which assess where learners need more help in specifically.

All measurement devices need to be valid. Thus, standardized tests, for example to be valid, should measure salient achievement in social studies content and not in another academic discipline. It must not posses test items which contain highly complex words and thus become a test of reading abilities.

To be reliable, the test needs to measure consistency of pupil test results. Both validity and reliability data are provided in the Manual for the adopted test.

Conclusion

Relevant facts, concepts and generalizations must be chosen as objectives for pupil achievement. Aligned learning opportunities with a variety of activities stresses indepth teaching. Evaluation procedures should be varied and assist in ascertaining pupil progress.

REFERENCES

Ediger, Marlow (2009), "Issues in the Social Studies," Experiments in Education, 37 (4), 75-78.

Ediger, Marlow, and D. Bhaskara Rao (2012), Essays in Teaching Social Studies. New Delhi, India: Discovery Publishing House.

CHAPTER 20

Science, Scope and Sequence Revisited

Scope and sequence, in any academic discipline, needs to be studied and modifications made where necessary. Science is no exception since trends and issues change in time and place. There have been numerous studies made and recommendations have then come about due to changes which need to be made. Various research and study groups have advocated innovations and change.

Scope and Sequence in Science

Scope answers the broad question of ***what*** should be taught in science units of study. The breadth of content and skills is then stated as guidelines for science teachers to follow in teaching and learning situations. Deliberation and indepth study are necessary. A flexible plan for the scope of science units of study for the knowledge and concepts area should include he following:

- relevant facts and ideas.
- understandings of vital concepts, generalizations, and main ideas.
- analyzing subject matter in terms of facts versus opinions, accurate versus inaccurate content, as well as the relevant from the irrelevant.
- synthesizing subject matter which ties together that which survives analyzation.
- evaluation in accordance with what is useful, as in subject matter for problem solving.

Subject matter objectives and learning opportunities are one and need to be integrated. Learning opportunities for pupils are there to achieve objectives of instruction. Learners are of different interests, capacities, and talents; thus, the science teacher must provide for individual differences. Subject matter taught must be meaningful to the pupil. He/ she must understand that which is taught, be it inductively or deductively. Science teachers need to assist learners to perceive purpose or reasons for achieving. If purpose is lacking, motivation will go downhill in attaining science objectives. With motivation, an increased energy level for learning tends to accrue; waiting for weekends to occur or school to be let out for the day is then minimized. Eagerness for achievement within a specific learning opportunity provides opportunities for growth, rich experiences, and extension. Science teachers, too, need to select those activities which not only assist in objectives achievement, but also create enthusiasm for learning with a child centered science curriculum being in evidence.

The total child needs to be considered when developing the science curriculum. Adequate nutritional needs must be met with high quality school lunches and breakfasts, as well as take home food for the weekend. A weakness exists in meeting dinner needs of leaners; perhaps after school programs with extended learnings in science, followed by an evening meal would be in order. Hungry children cannot succeed well in the school setting and nutrition needs must be met.

There are children who lack suitable clothing which a school can provide. School principals in a smaller district worked cooperatively in getting good, used clothing for pupils as these were needed. To provide decent, safe shelter for needy children is, perhaps, beyond the boundaries of responsibilities, but is necessary in assistance for some children.

In the school setting, children, children need to feel safe from harmful intruders. Emergency plans need to be worked out to keep any form of violence and abuse out. Getting safely to and from school is an obligation which must be met.

To attain well in science, the total child needs consideration. For example, hungry children do not do well in school or in society.

Learning Opportunity Emphasis

Science experimentation should be at the heart of the curriculum. Here, pupils with teacher guidance devise sequential experiments cooperatively. Social development is stressed in these learning opportunities. Pupils need to be focused here and work collaboratively. Good human relations must be in evidence whereby each participant shares ideas in working for the good of all. No one should be shunned or ridiculed, and each is accepted with feelings of belonging. Pupils are aided to be successful in ongoing activities. Each experiment must have a clearly defined problem with accompanying related hypotheses. The hypotheses individually are subject to testing to see if they are relevant and cogent. Hypotheses may be accepted, modified, or refuted, depending upon their findings. A variety of reference sources might well be utilized as data sources to secure information and these include the following: internet sources, vital videos, textbooks and workbooks, and technological sources in general.

Grouping procedures are salient in teaching and learning situations. There has been considerable debate on homogeneous versus heterogeneously grouping of pupils for instruction. This might be resolved in part by raising the question, "Under which conditions do pupils learn best in science?" In reading science content, for example, the science teacher might desire to group those pupils needing the most assistance separately so that needs are met in the following areas:

- word identification and recognition. In dealing with the abstract, selected pupils experience a plethora of difficulties. Here, context clues may be very helpful to the learner. If this is not adequate, phonic analysis may be added in ascertaining unknown words.
- the text selection read collectively with the teacher. Thus, pupils might follow along in their own texts as they read aloud together. In this way, recognizing the unknown is not a major problem.
- discussions leading to higher levels of cognition. Too frequently, the lower levels of thinking are stressed such

as recall of facts. Rather, pupils should think critically and creatively pertaining to subject matter encountered. Accuracy of content then is desired whereby learners come up with content suitable for scientific thought. Through scaffolding, science teachers might well assist pupils to come up with carefully examined principles and hypotheses.

- electronic science books whereby pupils read successfully in word recognition and vocabulary development (Ediger, 2014).

Assessing Pupil Achievement

There are numerous approaches in evaluating learner progress. Teacher observation is rather continuous and the science teacher might well notice pupil engagement in ongoing activities, attitudes toward learning, as well as retention of knowledge, and skills. Records may be kept and dated to refer to when making comparisons of observations made. Additional information of learner achievement in objectives attainment may come through:

- mandated test results in science.
- teacher devised test results.
- pupil products such as the quality of projects completed individually as well as within a committee.
- working effectively with others (Ediger and Rao, 2013).

Conclusion

In designing the science curriculum in terms of scope and sequence, science teachers need to study and appraise the objectives section carefully. Learning opportunities need to align with the objectives of instruction. Evaluation is necessary to ascertain if the stated objectives have been attained by pupils.

REFERENCES

Ediger, Marlow (2014), "Reading, Science, and the Pupil," Connecticut Journal of Science Education, 51 (2), 5-7.

Ediger, Marlow, and D. Bhaskara Rao (2013), Essays in Teaching Science. New Delhi, India: Discovery Publishing House.

CHAPTER 21

Motivating Pupils in Science Activities

With an increased emphasis upon teaching science, it behooves teachers to be highly proficient in teaching subject matter as well as in appropriate use of methods of instruction. Pupil achievement is always being challenged to achieve at a higher level. This is noticeable when comparisons are made among states in the nation as wells internationally. Thus, teachers of science must be well trained to provide for individual differences among pupils involving interests, talents, as well as abilities. Continuous teacher growth needs to be stressed within the framework of inservice education. Self efficacy of science teachers, as goal, motivates individuals to take advantage of the numerous opportunities available to grow, develop, and achieve as professionals. Personal effort is needed as a motivator (Ediger and Rao, 2012).

Motivating Pupils to Achieve in Science

The psychology of education has valuable concepts to offer science teachers in assisting improved pupil achievement. It is poignant to secure active pupil engagement in ongoing lessons and units of study. Opposite of active engagement is passive acceptance of subject matter presented which greatly limits pupils in realizing more optimal progress. Within each lesson, pupils need to build a solid base of facts, concepts, and generalizations, useful in subsequent lessons. These learnings then guide pupils to attain a sequence of experiences which might well be utilized in a spiral science curriculum. Revisits of content is then possible, but at more complex levels of thinking. Thorough pupil involvement in each learning opportunity is necessary in order the pupil does well in science.

Second, higher levels of cognition must be stressed in ongoing lessons and units of study. Inquiry methods should permeate instruction and resonate throughout the science curriculum. Probing and critical thinking are then in the offing. Inquiry methods provide excitement for learners in making discoveries, leading on to other activities with enthusiasm. Science experiments, a major part of the curriculum, provide excellent settings for enthusiasm in learning by discovery. Experiments and their planning should involve pupils with teacher leadership. Here, all can observe the experiment carefully in developing an hypothesis to a problem. Each hypothesis needs recording so that it can be tested within the experiment and through the utilization of related reference materials. Jumping to hasty conclusions when conducting experiments must be avoided; rather, careful observation, discussion, and reflection in thinking might result in modification, and change of the original hypothesis. There is excitement and enthusiasm in experimentation and testing hypotheses.

A third principle of learning from educational psychology stresses learner purpose in each learning opportunity. Establishing purpose within pupils assists in providing higher energy levels for achievement. Learners need to feel that ongoing learning opportunities have value and are useful in school and in society. Acquiring content for the sake of doing so will not cut it. Rather, intrinsically pupils feel the saliency of facts, concepts, and generalizations being stressed in each science lesson. In supervising university student teachers in the public schools, the writer noticed different procedures used by student/cooperating teachers in helping pupils see relevance of subject matter being acquired. Those who truly emphasized the importance of pupils to perceiving relevancy in ongoing units of study tended to increase motivation within learners. More pupil effort is then put forth in attaining objectives of instruction.

Fourth, meaning attached to content learned is vital in that pupils then understand ensuing subject matter. Initial learnings must become a part of learner repertoire in order to understand subsequent facts, concepts, and generalizations. If a pupil misses out on attaching meaning to pervious learnings presented, there will be an empty space in sequential learnings. This empty space needs to be taken care of regardless of why a pupil missed out on a previous lesson or lessons. Special care must be provided by the teacher in taking care of the deficiencies since new subject matter will be built upon previously presented ideas.The science teacher must be a good diagnostician in ascertaining what specifically is lacking in sequential learnings. Increased motivation occurs when pupils are able to sequence or order their very own learnings. A higher energy level for learning then comes into being when pupils:

- possess intrinsic motivation for achieving objectives.
- learn more optimally due to methodology utilized.
- evaluation results are used to improve instruction and not to minimize pupil progress.
- attach meaning to inherent subject matter.
- develop good attitudes toward the scientific method and science in general.

Fifth, the attitudinal dimension is emphasized in teaching and learning situations. Energy levels need to be upped with challenging, yet achievable knowledge and skills. An attitude of objectivity must prevail when engaging in ongoing lessons and units of study. Wholesome attitudes toward each other and toward committee and collaborative endeavours need to be in the offing. Pupils need to perceive practical applications of learnings acquired. There are a plethora of uses to be made of science subject matter. Technology is used to assist pupils to inquire, learn, and achieve. Numerous programs of instruction stress the saliency of utilization such as in STEM offerings.

In Closing

Motivation is a key factor in teaching and learning situations; Lent and Gilmore (2014), wrote the following ten standards for pupil motivation:

- active learning permeates instruction.
- lessons and projects incorporate student autonomy.
- relevance creates authentic purposes for learning.
- students have frequent opportunities for contributions.
- technology is used appropriately to increase learning opportunities and indepth study.
- multiple learning activities create opportunities for intellectual growth.
- the right balance of success and challenge creates a climate for independence.
- differentiation and scaffolding ensure that every student has opportunities to learn well.
- feedback and authentic assessment create deep, sustained learning.
- inquiry creates a sense of curiosity and a desire to learn.

The Next Generation Science Standards (NGSS) provide valuable information for inservice education on objectives, learning opportunities, and appraisal procedures for teachers in teaching pupils in the school setting. These are indeed worthy of study, indepth thought, and possible implementation.

REFERENCES

Ediger, Marlow, and D. Bhaskara Rao (2012), Essays in Teaching Science. New Delhi, India: Discovery Publishing House.

Lent, Releah Cossett, and Barry Gilmore (2014), "10 Standards for Motivation," Educational Leadership 72 (1), 66-67

CHAPTER 22

Science, A Psychological Versus A Logical Approach in Teaching

Under which approach do pupils attain more optimally, a logical versus a psychological procedure of instruction? Pupils do need to achieve well in a world of science. Science is all around us and pupils need to understand various principles and laws of science. Thus, teachers in the school curriculum must choose carefully objectives for pupil attainment in each lesson and unit of study. The worth and value of each needs to be weighed in order to promote relevancy in science teaching and learning situations.

Science teachers are better educated than ever before with master's, specialists in education, as well as doctoral degrees. With essential knowledge of science subject matter and methods of teaching, the teacher is better prepared to enlist and encourage learning. However, too many pupils turn off in ongoing science lessons and units of study. In supervising university student teachers in the public schools, the writer observed pupils who were highly motivated as well as those who needed a shot in the arm to achieve vital objectives in science. A problem faced by all teachers is to develop and maintain pupils interest in learning. (Ediger and Rao, 2014).

A Logical Science Curriculum

Here, science teachers are at the center of the stage in teaching and learning situations. The philosophy being that the teacher is well grounded in knowledge and skills to select objectives of instruction, learning activities for pupils to achieve each objective, and evaluation techniques to ascertain progress, is at the heart of a logical approach of instruction. With the many facts, concepts, and generalizations attained in preparation for science teaching, as well as relevant inservice education experiences, A logical procedure seems to have much going for it.

The teacher is in a good position, here, to provide remedial instruction where necessary. Gaps in pupil learning may be filled in with teacher proficiency in knowledge and skills. Pupils might then move on in sequence to an ensuing lesson with adequate background information. Unfulfilled gaps hinder future achievement which is built upon what has been accomplished. Materials of instruction utilized by the teacher in pupil goal attainment consist of the following:

- carefully chosen basal textbooks. Each lesson is properly introduced by having learners view related illustrations in the text and from the teacher's files.
- viewing the new words from the text lesson on the chalk/whiteboard. Each word is meticulously identified in its contextual meaning as it pertains to the lesson. This aids pupils in not misidentifying words while reading.
- teachers answering pupil's questions pertaining to content read; verification might come from the text as well as other reference sources.
- the science teacher setting up experiments to amplify subject matter from the reading activity.
- the teacher demonstrating clearly in the experiment what pupils are to attain.
- good discipline is needed to help pupils in observing and clarifying content and in providing for a quality school environment.

The teacher tests pupils frequently, using multiple choice and essay test items, to ascertain what has been learned. Feedback is used to assist in developing quality remedial instruction in ongoing and future units of study.

Scheduling of time for elementary school science is devoted to an appropriate amount of time each day of teaching with science emphasized strictly as a separate subject; correlation and integration of subject matter from other disciplines is minimal. This is done for the following reasons:

- science as a separate academic area has its very own body of knowledge and skills.
- science has its own scope and sequence in the curriculum.
- science loses its importance if correlation and integration with other academic disciplines is stressed.
- the methods of science must be emphasized, solely, whereby pupils work as professional scientists.
- the teacher determines which objectives to stress, the order of and which learning experiences to provide learners.
- valid and reliable means of appraising achievement and progress is determined by the science teacher (Ediger, 2008-2009).

A Psychological Science Curriculum

Here, the science teacher desires to have pupil involvement, as much as feasible, in determining sequence in ongoing units. Due to strong expertise in science knowledge and skills possessed, the teacher serves as a guide, a motivator, and encourages sequential achievement. Thus, the project method is utilized whereby pupils are motivated and encouraged to raise questions and problems. Background experiences from a variety of AV aids assists pupils in selecting a project to develop and complete. Thus, pupils perceive a ***purpose*** in the chosen project(s). Planning to achieve the purpose is involved. Committees of four members each, serve to plan collaboratively what the project will be as well as how to proceed in its fulfillment. Proper, flexible rules make it possible for pupils to respect each other as well being personally responsible for achievement. As a supervisor, the science teacher observes/helps pupils in making progress in carrying out plans for project completion. This leads to evaluation of the completed project with criteria such as the following agreed upon standards:

- quality of questions/problems raised by pupils.
- effort put forth by each committee member.

- independence in doing the project with teacher leadership involved.
- neatness and completeness of the project.
- becoming proficient in discussions where interaction among learners is involved (Ediger and Rao, 2013).

A variety in kinds of projects may be chosen such as:

- experiments and demonstrations. These should be considered as a major project to be completed, with a write-up of its essential parts and conclusion.
- doing a model of what was emphasized as a concept within a science unit of study, such as soil erosion.
- conducting a research study on a salient topic, such as causes and remediation of pollution in a local creek.
- collecting news items and displaying a persistent current events concern e. g., climate change.
- stressing STEM generalizations as in constructing a robot.

Comparing a Logical Versus a Psychological Science Curriculum

A logical approach in teaching emphasizes the teacher playing a leading role in selecting learning opportunities for pupils whereas the psychological curriculum stresses more of pupil input into curriculum development. Sequence in pupil learning is largely determined by the teacher in a logical approach, as compared to the science teacher assisting pupil to make choices in sequential learning opportunities. The scope in a science unit is ascertained by the teacher whereas scope is determined in part by pupils with teacher supervision in a psychological procedure. Available technology in its use is integrated, logically, by the science teacher as needed in aiding learner achievement in unit teaching as contrasted with its implementation through teacher/pupil planning in a psychological approach.

Many science teachers will use a blended procedure involving both a logical and psychological curriculum. Meeting the needs of pupils to achieve more optimally in science is a major objective and goal of instruction. Providing for individual differences is a necessity.

REFERENCES

Ediger, Marlow, and D. Bhaskara Rao (2014), Curriculum of School Subjects, Issues and Concerns. New Delhi, India: Discovery Publishing House.

Ediger, Marlow, and D. Bhaskara Rao (2013), Essays in Teaching Science. New Delhi, India: Discovery Publishing House.

Ediger,Marlow (2008-2009), Portfolios in Science, Connecticut Journal Of Science Education, 47(1), 28-29.

CHAPTER 23

Agriculture/Science Instruction, and Stem in Schools

With the broadening of the scope of science units, agriculture becomes highly salient. Farming is based upon science learnings due to, for example, in increasing crop and livestock yields and production. Productivity continues to increase in amount. Benjamin Franklin in the later 1700s commented on how hard farmers had to work to secured a small amount of grain. Presently, it becomes a problem of over production instead. Why has this occurred? Inventions, technology, and science have entered in to bring about these strong yields. There are numerous kinds of farms which specialize such as cattle, hog complexes, and grain emphasis. This manuscript basically will deal with the latter.

Agriculture, Technology, Inventions, and Science

Less two percent of public school students live and are raised on farms. At the time of the Revolutionary War in 1776, approximately 95% of the population made their livelihood from farming. Most public school students, presently, have very little knowledge about how farming has changed and tend to have little knowledge of the essentials of food and fiber production. The roles of technology has been tremendous. The writer grew up on a farm consisting of 160 acres. This was in a strong General Conference Mennonite community in which my father had grave reservations of my leaving the farm to attend college, beginning in 1949 and as time went on to became Professor of Education at a state university. I have always remained highly interested in changes in farming over the years and when attending a state fair always looked carefully at farm machinery innovations of which there were many. My only brother always remained a farmer and made his entire living from the farm; very few did that then nor do that today. His son farms the home place with four hundred acres of tillable land and also has a job in a nearby city. Many famers have part time or full time jobs in nearby small cities.

Farming in the 1930s and 1940s was rather primitive as compared to today. In 1935, draft horses were used to pull harrows to smooth and level the farm land for seeding crops. The farmer would walk in back of the harrow, holding the reigns in guiding the horses. In just a few years, hitches were put onto harrows to be pulled by tractors, usually on steel wheels which made for very rough riding experiences indeed! Draft horses for farming became a thing of the past. Still in the late 1930s and early 1940s rubber tires replaced the steel wheels which made for much smoother riding on tractors. On our farm, we had a new 1938 tractor to pull implements. The tractor was cranked and started with a crank, not a starter. A few farmers were injured when cranking by hand since the crank could quickly swing back briefly and rapidly in motion. Again, in a few years electric starters were built into tractors. With more acres being farmed per person, electric lights on the tractor came into being in the early 1940s which made it possible to harrow, disk, and plow land, late in the evening and throughout the night hours.

It was very difficult to attach some farm implements onto the tractor; thus in the early 1950s, the three point hitch came on the farming scene. The three point hitch on tractors made it possible to use hydraulic lifts to put plows into the ground for plowing as well as lift them out of the ground. Farm implements could then be driven on roads in moving from one piece of land to the next, without damaging the roads. Three point hitches, also made it much easier to attach implements to the tractor (Ediger and Rao, 2012).

Now, it is time to bring in air conditioned cabs into the discussion. My farmer brother had trouble with skin cancer and the dermatologist stated that he get an air conditioned cab for his tractor or quit farming. What an edict! He loved farming and that is what he had being doing all of his life. He lacked the money to buy the cab and air conditioning to put on his tractor, so he went into debt doing so. Fortunately, the farm crops did well the next summer so he could see the light at the end of the tunnel in paying for the innovation. I, myself, see a dermatologist several times a year; the reason being sun damage to my skin as a young person living on the farm.

Until a few years ago, farmers would plow their fields after harvest time. A depth of six to eight inches in depth was plowed resulting in the top soil being turned over. Now, no till farming is in vogue in that crops, like wheat, are seeded without ploughing the fields after harvest time. No till farming may involve disking the land once to kill weeds. Chemicals, such as herbicides, are also utilized to kill weeds. There are advocacy groups which desire organically processed foods whereby no farm chemicals have been used to spray crops. This would include growth hormones in livestock feed.

Seeding of farm crops occurs in late September, generally, for wheat. Com and soybeans are seeded in spring, after the winter temperatures have moderated to warmer spring temperature readings. Seeding with a modern grain drill, attached to and pulled by a tractor with a hydraulic lift, is done with a minimum of human effort. The grain to be seeded is augured from a truck into the drill box with the drill having a three point hydraulic hitch so it can be easily used in drilling seed as well as being transported by a tractor on roads to be taken to more distant areas for seeding. With no till farming, the residue from the previous crop stays on top of the soil and prevents soil erosion from heavy rainfalls, in particular. Also, if the wind is very strong, young wheat plants may blow out of their attachment to the ground, unless the residue prevents this from happening.

Usually, the latter days of June emphasize the harvesting of wheat. Modern self propelled combines with air conditioned cabs make harvesting easier, cleaner, and more comfortable.

Going back to the West Bank of the Jordan, then a part of the nation of Jordan in the early 1950s, a villager used a knife to cut the stalks of wheat and then wrapped a strand of wheat around these stalks to make a bundle. These bundles were placed on a threshing floor which is a hard surface of bare ground. To trample out the wheat in separating it from the chaff and straw, the villager had a donkey attached to a wooden "sled" which then trampled out the grain. The grain was then picked up with a crude wooden shovel and placed into a large wooden bowl, a highly labour intensive procedure.

In the late 1930s and early 1940s, the writer helped on the home farm by riding on a grain binder, pulled by a tractor; previously a team of draft horses was utilized to pull the grain binder. Cyrus Hall McCormick invented the first grain binder in 1837. This cut the number needed in harvesting from 7 to 4 workers. The grain binder cut the wheat and made bundles wrapped around with twine. A bundle carrier would carry the bundles until the carrier was "tripped," releasing approximately ten bundles to be "shocked," or set up by workers in a shock with the heads placed upward for drying by sunlight. About two months later, the shocks were loaded onto a wagon, with the use of a pitch fork and human muscle. This, indeed, was very labour intensive with the wagon filled with bundles being pulled by a tractor to a stationary threshing machine. Then the bundles were pitched individually from the wagon into the threshing machine which separated the grain from the straw and chaff. The grain then was moved from the threshing machine to a trailer to be shoveled into a grain bin. Shoveling wheat by hand was very difficult and tiring.

It was a great relief to farmers when the pull type combine arrived on the scene in the middle 1930s. The pull type was pulled by a tractor: it cut the grain blowing the stalks and chaff on the ground with the wheat being elevated to the grain bin on the machine. After a binfull had been cut, it was unloaded, gravity flow, onto a small truck, called a pickup. Generally, fifty bushels were loaded and then taken to a grain elevator, which purchased the grain. The grain elevator was located near to the local farm. It was not long, perhaps in the early 1950s, when the self propelled combine arrived on the scene. No tractor was needed since the machine and the threshing component were all one in the self propelled combine. The unloading augur on the side of the bin made it so that farmers could unload the binful of grain and keep driving/harvesting with the truck moving beside the self propelled combine. These combines were small initially with a 14 foot wide swath of grain to be cut at one time. The largest self propelled combine now can cut a forty foot wide swath with an eighteen wheeler truck, holding approximately 1,000 bushels of wheat/grain, now hauling the commodity to market at a grain elevator. Innovations have made it possible to farm larger acreages with few farmers needed (Ediger, 2010). This is far removed from the grain binder, with its shocking and threshing of bundles. Then too, with the grain augur, attached to the bin of a self propelled combine, auguring the grain onto a truck and then hauling the grain to an elevator in a nearby small city has made it so that the hand shovel is outdated. How tedious it was to shovel grain by hand. My nephew who farms the home place is taking a physical fitness course to regulate his body weight. No longer does the manual labour keep down the excessive body weight. With all the labour saving devices, farmers, too, can become overweight!

REFERENCES

Ediger, Marlow, and D. Bhaskara Rao (2012), Essays in Teaching Science. New Delhi, India: Discovery Publishing House.

Ediger, Marlow (2010, "Children's Literature in the Science Curriculum," Journal of Instructional Psychology, 37 (2), 117-119.

The Internet contains a plethora of pictures pertaining to topics discussed. For example, type in "grain binder" in a search engine such as Google, and see illustrations on horse drawn as well as tractor drawn (all on steel wheels). In 1941, I received 30 cents an hour working on a binder pulled by a tractor with rubber tires.

CHAPTER 24 Mathematics Achievement and the Pupil in School Setting

How might pupil achievement in mathematics be more Optimal and Yet be Enjoyable at the same time? This is a question which needs careful consideration in curriculum development. Much thought, research, and indepth searching for solutions to the problem must be forthcoming. Mathematics teachers working individually as well as in teams might well come up with answers and suggestions to problematic situations. The mathematics curriculum is subject to modification and change as innovative ideas accrue in a changing society.

Assisting Pupils to Achieve

Mathematics teachers need to study, indepth, objectives for learner attainment involved in mandated testing. These objectives provide needed information on the scope of the curriculum. Each objective, then, must be considered carefully in terms of meaning and implications for teaching. Understanding of these objectives are musts in mathematics curriculum improvement. Inservice education endeavours may help in these situations in listening to peers state their interpretations and means of implementation. Vagueness is minimized under these circumstances. Each objective needs careful scrutiny with the intent of guiding more optimal leaner progress.

Second, principles of learning from educational psychology need infusion into the instructional arena. There are selected agreed upon principles which teachers need to discuss and use in new situations. A major principle is to garner pupil involvement in ongoing activities and experiences. Too frequently, selected pupils are passive and do not participate mentally, perhaps waiting for the school day to end, and yet each period devoted to mathematics instruction is valuable. Ensuing learnings build upon those previously acquired, and if a pupil misses out due to ineffective behaviours, he/she fails in developing sequential learnings. Thus, active participation by each pupil is needed in ongoing lessons to build a repertoire of understandings. When pupils miss a day of school for whatever reason, they lose out on becoming increasingly proficient in mathematics. The lost learnings need to be taken care of through high quality relevant experiences. No pupil should fall through the cracks.

Pupil purpose in mathematics, too, enters into the equation. With purpose, learners accept reasons for achieving any objective. If there is a lack of purpose, the tendency will be for motivation to decrease in achievement. A purpose emphasizing drill and practice, alone, will not get the job done, but rather rich experiences in mathematics need to be ongoing. What is salient now, might not be relevant in the distant future. Pupils, then, need to perceive that what is acquired can be utilized in school and in society, presently as well as in the future. Too frequently, mathematics teachers fail to stress the poignancy of learner purpose in ongoing activities. As university supervisor of student teachers in the public schools for thirty years, the writer noticed time and again how important purpose in learning is to any pupil. Purpose truly is a motivator to achieve in mathematics, and pupils need to notice presently how mathematical subject matter being stressed in a lesson may be used within diverse situations. The teacher needs to model and demonstrate this usage.

Within objectives being emphasized in teaching and learning situations, the pupil must attach meaning to ongoing experiences. It is indeed frustrating to the learner if he/she does not understand content being taught. Many times, the pupil attempts to memorize subject matter being taught. But, this fails to provide a sound background of facts, concretes, and generalizations in order to attach meaning to subsequent leanings. Better it is if pupils understand each sequential step of learning, resulting in a solid foundation of experiences.

Teacher observation of learner progress must be stressed continuously, catching mathematical errors before they are practiced and become permanent in the child's repertoire. When a pupil explains orally how a word problem was solved, the mathematics teacher listens carefully/respectfully and changes/modifies learner comments when errors tend to accrue in these situations. Or when errors are made in basic arithmetic facts, the teacher might well assist in making for correct understandings through concrete activities. It might be necessary to go back to the use of manipulative materials, for example, to guide pupil understanding of the commutative property of addition. Additional evaluations made through teacher observation involving diagnosis include the following:

- time on task in working on an assignment.
- utilizing technology appropriately.
- working effectively in collaborative situations.
- completing work on time.
- using teaching aids when necessary.
- motivation to do mathematics for extra credit.

For each of the above asterisked items, the mathematics teacher needs to provide leadership and guidance so that pupils become increasingly independent learners. Pupil growth in achieving objectives is salient (Ediger, 2013).

Inservice Education in the Mathematics Curriculum

There are a plethora of opportunities in inservice education for mathematics teachers to increase proficiency in teaching and learning situations as well as to develop self efficacy. Teachers of mathematics may organize a series of professional meetings to improve the curriculum, centered around an agreed upon theme. With varying strengths and talents involved, each teacher may specify what he/she is strong in and would like to contribute. The meetings are centered around teacher purpose, need, and strength. Thus, a survey may be conducted listing possibilities on a checklist with a space included to indicate an open ended possibility. The format of the inservice program might well include seminars, small group committee endeavours, project methods, and demonstrations, among other creative possibilities. Ample materials must be available for each presentation with teachers discussing needs which they perceive in improving instruction. Inservice education goals should include the following in meeting needs of instruction:

- use of technology to solve problems in teaching.
- assisting pupils in problem solving.
- identifying pupil learning styles to provide for individual differences.
- recognizing creative behaviors and guiding learners to utilize these behaviors in the curriculum.

Different schools of thought need to be utilized in teaching mathematics in emphasizing purpose in ongoing lessons and units of study. Thus, the following may be identified and unitized in the math curriculum:

- measurable stated objective when basic addition, subtraction, multiplication, and division facts are stressed.
- problem solving when deliberation and thought goes into finding solutions to lifelike and simulated word problems.
- novelty and uniqueness of endeavors when ascertaining and speculating on possible answers to questions.
- reading mathematical content literally versus using figurative expressions.
- project methods in using constructivism as a philosophy of education.
- collaborative work when stressing social development within the framework of achieving mathematical subject matter (Ediger, 2006).

In addition to local teacher developed leadership methods of inservice education, mathematics etchers individually might wish to work on or complete a graduate degree in mathematics education. The course/courses taken from an accredited university must meet needs of the mathematics teacher. Thus, relevancy is a key concept here in that learnings acquired must asset the teacher to become proficient and grow in self efficiency.

Course work taken needs to assist the teacher to possess a strong background of subject matter knowledge which relates rather directly to teaching and learning situations in the classroom. A sound basis of subject matter knowledge helps the teacher to diagnose pupil difficulties more readily and provide remedies which work. Also in graduate course work taken, the classroom teacher experiences diversity of methodology, applicable to teaching and learning situations. These methodologies must stress providing for individual differences among learners, such as interests, abilities, effort put forth, as well as for pupil objectives in life's endeavors in the societal arenas.

Conclusion

Motivation is a key component in stressing pupils achievement and progress in mathematics. It needs continuous emphasis as learners pass through the public school years. Lent and Gilmore (2014) list the following standards for motivation:

- active learning permeates instruction.
- lessons and projects incorporate student autonomy.
- relevance creates authentic purposes for learning.
- students have frequent opportunities for collaboration.
- multiple learning methods create opportunities for intellectual growth.
- the right balance of challenge and success creates a climate for independence.
- differentiation and scaffolding ensure that every student has opportunities to learn well.
- feedback and authentic assessment create deep sustained learning.
- inquiry promotes a sense of curiosity and a desire to learn.

REFERENCES

Ediger, Marlow (2013), "Teacher Observation to Evaluate Mathematics Achievement," Delta K (51), 1, 4-6.

Ediger, Marlow (2006), "Teaching Mathematics in the High School Setting," College Student Journal, 39 (4), 711 -716.

Lent, ReLeah Cossett, and Barry Gilmore (2014), "10 Standards for Motivation, 11 Educational Leadership, 72 (1), 66-67.

Index

O

P

Q

R

S

T

V

W

Z